# MERCURY COUGAR 1967-1987

## Produced by the Staff of Automobile Quarterly

# MERCURY COUGAR 1967-1987

## By Gary Witzenburg

**Produced by the Staff of Automobile Quarterly**

**AUTOMOBILE QUARTERLY PUBLICATIONS**

**VICE PRESIDENT AND PUBLISHER:** RICHARD A. BARTKUS
**FOUNDING PUBLISHER:** L. SCOTT BAILEY

**EDITORIAL STAFF**
**EDITOR-IN-CHIEF:** THOS L. BRYANT
**EDITOR:** LOWELL C. PADDOCK
**MANAGING EDITOR:** CHRISS BONHALL
**ASSOCIATE EDITOR:** JOHN F. KATZ
**ASSOCIATE EDITOR:** JULIE M. FENSTER
**ART DIRECTOR:** MICHAEL PARDO
**ASSOCIATE ART DIRECTOR:** DAVID W. BIRD II
**CHIEF PHOTOGRAPHER:** ROY D. QUERY
**BUSINESS SERVICES DIRECTOR:** FRED BAILEY
**PRODUCTION DIRECTOR:** LOU JOHNSON
**PRODUCTION MANAGER:** KAREN L. SINRUD
**BUSINESS MANAGER:** KEVIN G. BITZ
**MARKETING DIRECTOR:** STEPHEN E. PEARSON

**EDITOR FOR THIS BOOK:** LOWELL C. PADDOCK
**ART DIRECTOR:** DAVID W. BIRD II

**CBS MAGAZINES, A DIVISION OF CBS INC.**
**EXECUTIVE STAFF**
**PRESIDENT:** PETER G. DIAMANDIS
**VP, EDITORIAL DIRECTOR:** CAREY WINFREY
**SENIOR VP, PUBLISHING:** ROBERT F. SPILLANE
**SENIOR VP, CIRCULATION:** ROBERT ALEXANDER
**SENIOR VP, OPERATIONS & ADMINISTRATION:** ROBERT J. GRANATA
**VP, FINANCE:** ARTHUR SUKEL
**VP, SUBSCRIPTION CIRCULATION:** BERNARD B. LACY
**VP, MANUFACTURING & DISTRIBUTION:** MURRAY M. ROMER
**PRESIDENT, CBS MAGAZINE MARKETING:** CARL KOPF

Typesetting by Computer Typesetting Services, Inc., Glendale, California. Color separations by Phototype Color Graphics, Pennsauken, New Jersey; American Color Corp., Santa Ana, California; and South China Printing Co., Hong Kong. Printing and binding by South China Printing Co., Hong Kong Editorial offices: 1499 Monrovia Ave., Newport Beach, California 92663; (714) 720-5300. ©1987 by CBS Magazines, a division of CBS Inc. Reproduction without permission is prohibited. Library of Congress Catalog Number 87-70752 ISBN 0-915038-63-3. AUTOMOBILE *Quarterly* and ⊛ are registered trademarks of CBS Inc. All rights reserved under Pan American and Universal Copyright Conventions by CBS Inc.

# INTRODUCTION

Bryar Park, New Hampshire, August 6, 1967, the Bryar 250. The big guns in Trans-Am are there: Mustang, Cougar, 911 and Camaro. A light drizzle at the beginning of the race becomes a downpour. With most of the cars running on slicks, the fray quickly turns dangerous, as drivers test the limits of their skills and their cars. It is only a matter of time before fate enters the equation. It starts when Mustang driver Ken Duclos slams into teammate Jerry Titus, knocking both out of the race. Ed Leslie, a Cougar driver, is running rain tires and moves into

the lead but falters with a blown engine. Peter Revson, another Cougar driver, prevails over Bert Everett's 911 and takes the win. It is now halfway through the 12-race 1967 season, and the Mercury Cougar team is in the lead with 39 points to the Mustang's 34.

Looking back from our 20-year vantage point, it may come as a surprise that the Mercury Cougar played such a strong role in the 1967 Trans-Am season. After all, the Cougar wasn't really intended to be an all-out performance car; its mandate was to blend performance *and* luxury, to be an American interpretation of a European GT. Yet to demonstrate that its fledgling car had as much substance as style, Lincoln-Mercury hired Bud Moore of Spartanburg, South Carolina, to prepare a three-car team for an assault on the 1967 Trans-Am season. With such skilled drivers as Dan Gurney, Ed Leslie, Parnelli Jones, Peter Revson, LeRoy and Cale Yarborough and David Pearson, it was hardly an amateur venture. Considering that Team Cougar was up against a concerted effort from both the Shelby Mustangs (who no doubt had some official encouragement *not* to let the "smaller division" take too many checkered flags) and the likes of Mark Donohue, Vince Piggins and the Camaro Z-28, it was a fiercely fought contest.

In the end, the Over-2-Liter category was decided by a mere two points, and the Mustangs had them both. Team Cougar had been provided its opportunity in 1967, and Ford chose to focus on the Mustang team in 1968.

Despite its manifest competition record, Lincoln-Mercury continued to market its Cougar as a combination of show and go. "Cougar is a whole car full of luxury features from front to rear," said one early brochure. But models like the Dan Gurney Special, the XR7-G, the GT-E and the Eliminator earned a rightful place amongst their musclebound contemporaries, proving that the "Mustang with class" could flex some muscle as well. Yet the allusions to the Cougar's European inspiration were more than just ad copy. To see just how close to the target it came, *Popular Mechanics* asked race driver Roger Ward to compare the new Cougar with an Aston Martin DB-6 for its March 1967 issue. While the comparison may seem almost odious in hindsight, it spoke volumes about the attributes the Cougar was intended to possess. "For performance and luxury," wrote Ward, "I'd say the Cougar is a car for the man who aspires to own an Aston Martin, but hasn't got the pocketbook for it."

When the crunch came, with tighter emissions regulations, skyrocketing insurance rates and—ultimately—the energy crisis, Ford was forced to confront the Cougar's split personality. With gas in short supply, performance became far less critical than efficiency or luxury and Lee Iacocca ruled that the Mustang and Cougar, siblings under the skin, would go their separate ways. As the Cougar had never really been a true sports model, it seemed a wise decision to move it upscale, nudging it towards the Thunderbird and away from the now-shrunken Mustang.

This certainly was not an easy task, nor always a successful one. After all, Christopher the Cougar's snarl must have sounded a little tepid alongside a Cougar sedan or wagon. "We were a little concerned," recalled Ford designer Gail Halderman, "that the Cougar was losing its identity. . . . It was a bit of a struggle to do Cougar four-doors; and then, once we'd swallowed that, they said, 'OK, now we want you to make a wagon.'" That the Cougar was able to survive into the Eighties with elements of its image intact is a testament to the clever marketing techniques, such as Chauncey and Christopher the Cougar, that were used to develop its image.

The Cougar's complete rebirth in 1983 found it sharing the same relationship with the Thunderbird as it had had with the original Mustang. But in spite of the Thunderbird influence, the Cougar once again had a character of its own, with a clear marketing focus. Offered in a single body style, it attracted a willing audience that helped model year sales grow from 67,170 in 1982 to 115,546 in 1984.

For 1987, the Cougar's new identity is further burnished with the addition of a limited-production 20th Anniversary Edition. With its sumptuous leather interior, distinctive exterior appearance and powerful 5.0-liter H.O. V-8, the new Cougar offers a blend of performance and style, an Eighties analogy of its original identity.

*Mercury Cougar, 1967-1987* germinated as an article authored by Gary Witzenburg on the original 1967-1973 Cougars published in AUTOMOBILE *Quarterly* magazine. Given the increasing interest in the Cougar as a collectible automobile, it was only natural that the article be extended to book length. I am indebted to many in its production, and Gary is foremost among them for his willingness to seek out and interview those individuals involved with the Cougar throughout its 20-year history. I am also grateful to many individuals within Ford Motor Company who assisted with this project from the very start, including: John Aiken, Bill Buffa, Bonnie Daws, Charles W. Day, Chuck Gumushian, Gail Halderman, Rich Kuchinski, Eric Petersen, Paul Preuss, Mike Scott, Jerry Senior and Rick Squires. I also wish to acknowledge the personal involvement of John Baumann of the National Cougar Club who volunteered to drive his 1967 Dan Gurney Special to Ford's Dearborn Proving Ground in the dead of winter for the cover photograph. And *Road & Track*'s librarian, Otis Meyer—always the finder of the unfindable—came through with several rare photographs of prototype and racing Cougars. Thanks as well to photographers Roy D. Query, Leslie Bird and Bill Sumner who contributed their time and effort to produce work of the highest order.

Finally, I am indebted to those Cougar owners who allowed us to photograph their cars. They are a hardy bunch, these, for the Cougar still does not command the same respect among contemporary car collectors as does some of its less sophisticated competitors. Here's to hoping that time will justify their foresight.

**Lowell C. Paddock**
Newport Beach, California

# PART ONE: A CAT AMONG THE PONIES, 1967-1973

When Ford Division boss Lee Iacocca became impatient with Ford Styling's lack of progress on the small sporty car he was proposing to build and market, he and Styling Vice President Gene Bordinat proposed a contest. Three exterior studios—Ford, Lincoln-Mercury and Corporate Projects (Advanced)—drew up and sculpted two clay models each in a bit over two weeks, a then truly remarkable achievement.

Then, on a muggy mid-August morning in 1962, Iacocca and his staff reviewed the six candidates on a viewing patio behind the Ford Styling building in Dearborn. Not recorded in official Ford history is the fact that Iacocca was attracted at first to a racy-looking number from the Ford Studio called "Stiletto." When that design was later determined to be too pricey to build, however, he settled on the other Ford Studio candidate. A clean, mildly aggressive little car with an open-mouthed grille, a Thunderbirdesque notchback roof, simulated rear-quarter scoops and three-element vertical tail lamps, it was created by Assistant Ford Studio Chief David Ash under chief Designer Joseph Oros. And it became, of course, the 1965 Ford Mustang.

But an often-forgotten sidebar to the great Mustang success story is the fact that Ford's pioneer ponycar might well have been called the Cougar. That original, contest-winning Oros/Ash clay model was labeled Cougar and sported a graceful cat emblem in the center of its mouthy grille. Oros was adamant that the car be named Cougar and wrote several notes to Iacocca pressing his case. Everyone called it that throughout its early development, and various versions of Oros' Cougar cat design—all with its tail arched forward and one paw outstretched—were prepared for grille, fender, rear panel and wheelcover badges.

Later, when "Cougar" lost out first to "Torino," then (at the last minute) "Mustang" as the new baby Ford's name, Oros sent the full-size grille ornament from his original model to Iacocca. Attached to its back was a hand-lettered card reading: "This is to help you remember what we should have called the car."

Flash forward to the summer of 1964. Ford's Mustang, launched just that April, has captured young America's fancy and is fast becoming Ford Motor Company's most successful new model ever. Industry eyebrows are raised in awed surprise all across the Motor City, and faces are long at General Motors as the sporty Monza version of Chevrolet's rear-engine, six-cylinder Corvair is being soundly trounced in the showroom sales wars.

*Above: The 1962 Oros/Ash Mustang prototype was named "Cougar" and sported Cougar grille emblem. Below: Mustang-derived "T-7" Cougar prototype was constructed with a fiberglass front end grafted onto a Mustang body.*

Chevrolet General Manager and GM Vice President S. E. (Bunkie) Knudsen is pitching GM's brass for approval to get on the stick and design and develop a proper Mustang competitor. Pontiac Division Chief and GM Vice President Elliott (Pete) Estes is fruitlessly petitioning the same conservative bunch for permission to one-up both Ford and Chevy with an affordable two-seat sports car.

Across town in Dearborn, Lee Iacocca—who a year and a half earlier had had a terrible time selling his ponycar idea to Henry Ford II and other top execs—is promoted . . . to executive vice president with responsibility for all the company's North American passenger cars. Oros' Cougar emblem with note still attached makes the move with him from one desk to another (much larger) one.

Even before Iacocca's Mustang hit the streets, however, Ford's upscale Lincoln-Mercury Division had begun toying with the idea of a small

*Above: Another version of the Mustang-based T-7 prototype explored "electric shaver" grille treatment with concealed headlamps. Below: A fastback Cougar coupe was also considered in car's early development.*

*Above: Two 1965 clay models (top and middle) were merged to create final version from John Aiken's Advanced Studio (above). Below: Proposed Cougar rear bumper would turn up elsewhere in the Mercury lineup.*

sporty car of its own. Sketches showing the earliest beginnings of such a project date as far back as February 1963.

Less than 18 months later, with the Mustang well on its way to stardom and GM management about to approve what would become the rival Chevrolet Camaro, newly appointed Lincoln-Mercury Advanced Styling Studio Manager John Aiken was given the Mercury sporty coupe assignment. "There had already been a couple of false starts," he recalls. "One that I was involved in used a plastic add-on front end on a Mustang body. Everything from the windshield back was Mustang, but the front was fiberglass cappings." The reason behind such a radical approach, Aiken says, ". . . was to get something out there quickly." The material was FRP (fiberglass reinforced plastic), the stuff Corvettes had been made of for more than a decade.

But that idea, happily, had been dropped due to fit, finish, color-match-

*Four-door Cougar was considered as late as February, 1965.*

ing and plastic-to-metal bonding problems. Among other things, the FRP front fenders couldn't be made to look right with the metal Mustang doors. "Our technology at that time was not too great," Aiken says. "Of course, Corvettes weren't too wonderfully done in those days, either."

The Division decided then to "go all out," according to Aiken, and design a completely new body over the Mustang's inner structure; the windshield and roof rails would be the new car's only common exterior features. The idea was to position the car as a "luxury" sports coupe somewhere between the low-buck Mustang and the prestigious Thunderbird in size, image and price. The program's code name was "T-7" (the original Mustang had been "T-5"), and the eventual choice of a real name for Mercury's soon-to-be-upscale ponycar should have been practically preordained.

There followed another competition among three studios, this time with only one model apiece, and Aikeh's L-M Advanced Styling Studio entry won hands down. Well, not quite. "At one point there was a grille theme done by Dave Ash's Special Projects Studio that was different from ours," he explains. "Both had vertical grille bars, but theirs had a more upright front profile with the center nose. The final front end was a combination of our theme and theirs, but the rest of the car was ours."

As approved in February 1965, the final exterior design featured twin wide grilles of slim, protruding blades split by a body-color, sheetmetal nose. Headlamps were hidden, bumpers curved upward at their ends, and the subtly rounded sides were bordered by peaked front fenders flowing past the greenhouse into a rear-quarter kick-up above, and a reverse-rake character line below.

Several variations of this basic theme, including a flying-buttress fastback and a four-door sedan with T-Bird-type "landau" roof bars were evaluated on paper, and a convertible version was sculpted in clay; but only the original cleanly sculpted coupe would reach production a year and a half later. Aiken's stylists also experimented with a variety of grille, tail lamp and rear-bumper designs, before returning to the original split waterfalls in front; the same look was echoed in back with full-width bladed tail lamps divided by the combined license-plate holder and fuel-filler door.

Aiken relates that he and his team, working under the able direction of

*1967 Dan Gurney Special, owned by John and Dee Ann Baumann*

Lincoln-Mercury Chief Designer Buz Griesinger, were considerably influenced by European sedans of the time, especially the Mark X Jaguar. "European style has become kind of a buzzword today," he says, "almost equated with good design. But 20 years ago it was a bold new direction for us. The Mustang was very much an all-American sporty car, but we felt the Cougar should have more of a European look and image, more of that so-called continental flair."

"We looked very strongly at the Jaguar sedan, and we asked ourselves, 'What is the mystique of the Jaguar?' We wanted a car that, like the Jag, was curvaceous and feline in shape and form, with a highly sculpted look."

Aiken describes the design of the Cougar's sides as "one of the first pieces of metal where we really got into a high sculptural effect. The Mustang was very flat-sided with a depression through the door that terminated in a simulated scoop in front of the rear wheel. The idea with the Cougar, on the other hand, was to give it a very strong theme and a feeling of length. We wanted to make it look a bit longer than it really was to help separate it visually from the Mustang. Maximum differential from the Mustang was also the reason for the reverse-wedge lower character line along the side. The roof was essentially the same as the Mustang's except that our sail panels, or C-pillars, were more sculpted with a little bit of a trailing edge."

Like many Thunderbirds, Mercurys and other Ford products of the middle Sixties, the Cougar's nose was pointed in profile. Its rear deck was essentially flat with the peaked upper fenders forming vestigial fins at its outer ends. Then there were the gimmicky sequential taillights, inherited from the '65–'66 "Buck Rogers" T-birds. "That wasn't a Design Staff idea," says Aiken. "It came to us from someone in Electrical Engineering. They brought it in and asked if we wanted to use it. So I designed a mock-up, and we adapted our theme to it and incorporated it into our clay model.

"One day I was asked to come to Bordinat's office. So I went up there, very nervous, and he said, 'Nice job. I think we'll go with that.'

"We had a lot of team spirit in the studio in those days, and we were after anything that would make our car unique and different from the Mustang. We all thought it was great."

On the positive side, Aiken confirms that the '67 Cougar's interior was—like the exterior—influenced by Jaguar, which led to a good set of readable round gauges and later (in the mid-year, high-zoot XR-7 model) toggle-type switches and some fairly nice simulated burled walnut on the dash. "That was probably the first time we talked much about European design," he adds, "and the first time we cooperated fairly closely with the interior studio."

The earliest interior theme sketches had a strip-type speedometer above four small rectangle gauges. Then the small gauges became round, which led to four much larger, round, recessed gauges and ultimately to two large pods housing the speedometer and auxiliary read-

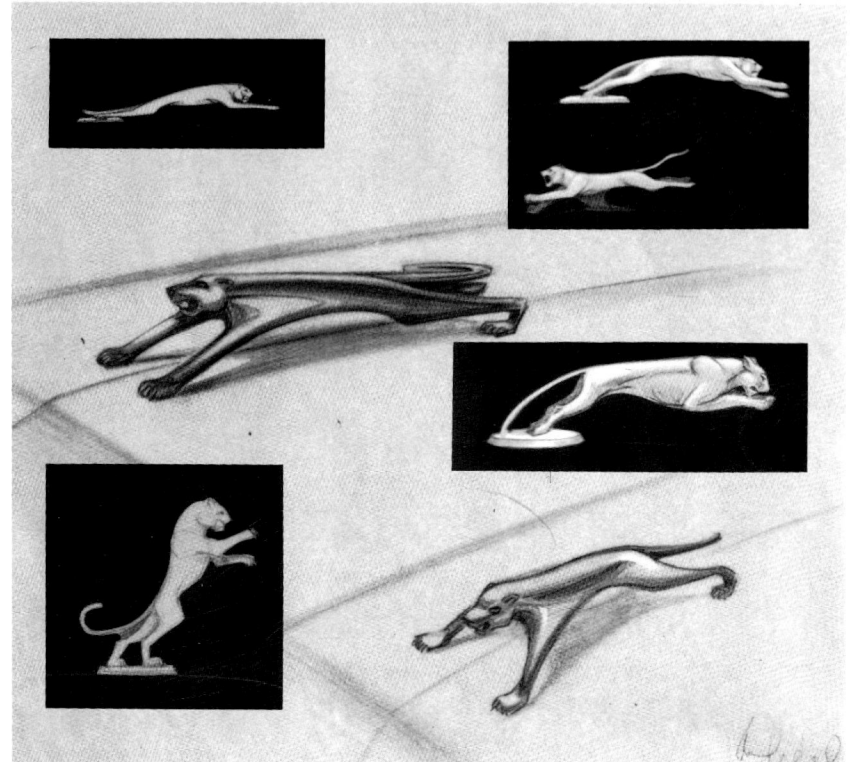

**Proposed Cougar emblems included a variety of static and leaping cats. Note resemblance to Jaguar's trademark feline.**

outs with a smaller round clock above and between them. The early horizontally ribbed panel design clashed badly with the vertical-blade front and rear exterior theme and was wisely discarded in favor of a much classier-looking (and safer) padded-vinyl appliqué.

When the Cougar was complete inside and out, Aiken recalls with pride that "... it had a more elegant, more classic look than the Mustang's. Even the other designers around here liked it a lot, and that doesn't always happen. It was a good feeling to have our co-workers appreciate the car as much as we did."

While the choice of the Cougar name probably *should* have been obvious, Mercury's marketing mavens insisted on playing their games with surveys and clinics and other suggested ideas. Among these were S-77, Apollo, Sceptre and even Lido, which just happens to be Lee Iacocca's real first name. But Cougar kept coming back at the top of the surveys, and the designers and most others at Ford had no doubt about what *they* wanted to call it.

"I think they named it Cougar because they had all the cats already

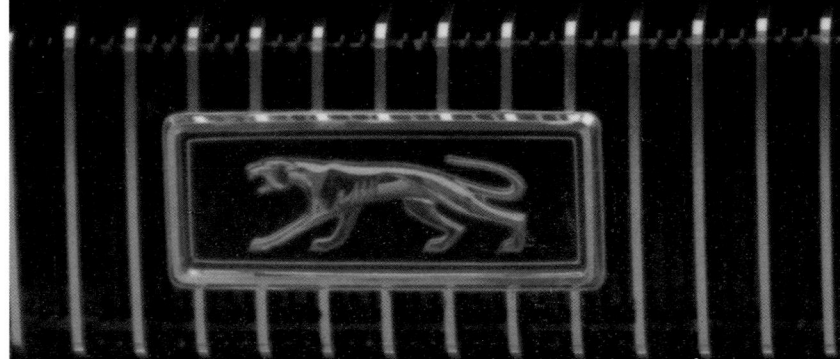

*Original grille emblem (top) was replaced by a more aggressive version (above); "Cougar" name was added later when Jaguar objected.*

designed," Iacocca joked years later, referring to the designers' earlier efforts at selling that name and symbol for what eventually became the Mustang. The fact is, the Cougar cat went through a thorough redesign from Oros' original stylized version to the meaner, more serious-looking snarling mountain lion that would later become the symbol of the entire Lincoln-Mercury Division.

Thoroughly unamused by all of this name and symbol finagling was Jaguar itself, which considered Mercury's Cougar cat a bit of a cheeky rip-off of its own leaping feline. At one point Jaguar even sued Ford Motor Company, claiming the Cougar's proposed grille emblem was too close to its own. L-M was eventually forced to add "Cougar" lettering beneath the prowling cat on the grille badges.

Underneath its classy body the '67 Cougar was basically standard-issue Mustang—except for a few details both major and minor. For one, it sat on a 111-inch wheelbase, 3 inches longer than the Mustang's (and 3.5 inches shorter than the Thunderbird's). For another, it featured an exclusive and fairly extensive, 123.5-pound sound-insulation package and a somewhat softer, better-controlled ride than the Mustang's. Both cars used the Falcon's double-control-arm front suspension, with a coil spring mounted on the upper arm, but unique to the Cougar was a new articulated drag strut that allowed the wheels to step back a bit on impact to reduce road shock. Its four-leaf rear springs were strapped to the solid axle with insulating "iso-clamps," and their front mounts were tied to the underbody through voided bushings for the same reason. Also, no six-cylinder engine was offered.

Both the base 289-cubic-inch two-barrel V-8 and an optional four-barrel version of the same engine came with single exhaust, the former rated at 200 horsepower, the latter at 225. The top power option was a beefy 390-cubic-inch four-barrel V-8 providing 320 horsepower—according to the optimistic "gross" power ratings of the time. It came with dual exhausts and (ordered as part of the GT performance group option) dual low-backpressure tuned resonators. Also included in the GT option were a performance handling package (stiffer springs, heavy-duty shocks and a larger front stabilizer bar), power front disc brakes (replacing the standard drums) and wide-oval whitewall tires on GT wheels.

Available transmissions were a standard three-speed manual, optional four-speed manual or three-speed Merc-O-Matic with the company's new "Select-Shift" feature. Unlike earlier Ford automatics, Select-Shift let drivers hold both first and second gears until they chose to upshift manually. The driver could also choose to start off in second for getting under way on slippery surfaces and manually downshift from third to second any time and from second to first at speeds below 25 mph. It was almost like driving a (clutchless) manual transmission, though not as efficient . . . or enjoyable.

The official Cougar launch was preceded by an elaborate and inventive six-month media campaign, the brainchild of then L-M Public Relations Director Gayle Warnock. Press releases were mailed from Cougar, Washington, and (at one point) from Hong Kong. "Cougar" burgers, a concoction of ground sirloin with a spicy additive and shaped to resemble a Cougar, were packed in dry ice and air-shipped to automotive editors and reporters across the country. (In at least one case, the recipient was out of town for several days, and his package became predictably aromatic.) These were followed by Cougar crackers, Cougar wine, Cougar fortune cookies and more, until no one in the auto-related media could have been unaware of the car's impending introduction.

Later, a spectacular press preview was held on board an amphibious landing craft off the beach at St. Thomas, in the Virgin Islands. And still later a young entertainer named Barbara McNair (remember her?) purred "Alley Cat" to a hundred auto writers assembled to test the car in Monterey, California.

Despite the growing crisis in Vietnam, the fall of 1966 was a relatively quiet and contented time, The Nixon presidency, Woodstock and the social upheaval of the later Sixties were still some time away. The top TV show was "Bonanza," the top football team, the Green Bay Packers, the

*Above: Cougar GT trim was evaluated on this early 1966 prototype. Below: Chauncey the Cougar remained the car's mascot until his death in 1975.*

number one song, "Cherish," by the Association.

And when the 1967 Cougar was introduced on September 30, 1966, it was hardly the only exciting new car in the showrooms. Among others were Chevy's rival Camaro, Ford's own restyled Mustang and Thunderbird, and Cadillac's all-new front-drive Eldorado. Mercury called its Cougar "America's first luxury/sports car at a popular price" and "a specialty car lithe in appearance with long hood and short deck testifying to the European flair of its styling." Its advertising dubbed it, simply, "Untamed elegance! . . . an entirely new kind of road animal from Mercury."

"Changes in car-buying tastes have occurred so rapidly in the past few years," stated Lincoln-Mercury Division General Manager and Ford Vice President Paul F. Lorenz on the occasion, "that it literally may be called a revolution. The sought-after qualities of today are grace, style, sophistication, quiet performance, luxury and understated elegance. The result is that the new specialty car market is increasing in size and importance because of the strong consumer demand to step up to something better in the personal car field.

"The Cougar is the only American market entry that has been developed specifically as a luxury sports car at a popular price with features and appointments that previously had been available only in the larger, more expensive American luxury/personal cars. The Cougar also offers responsive performance, refinement and understated elegance that rival

**1968 Cougar XR7-G, owned by Virgil and Wilma Brown**

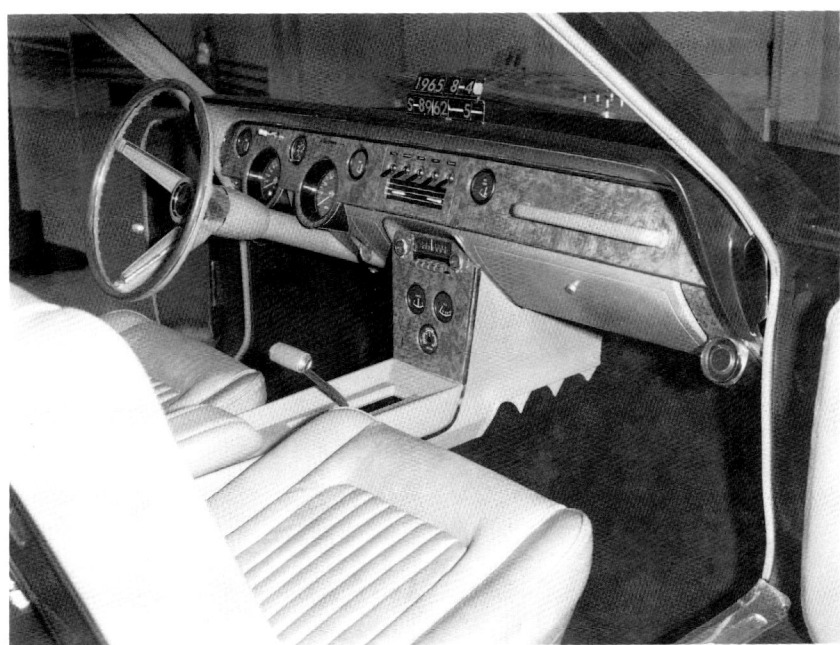

*Below: Early Cougar interior called for a horizontal, ribbed theme. Above and facing page: Later versions became more sophisticated; note Jaguar-style toggle switches. October 1965 version (opposite, left) bears "Lido" script on wheel.*

the best of the European road cars that are for more expensive to own and operate."

Let's sort out and examine a bit of that hyperbole. Features and appointments? Check. Given the sparse equipment levels of the standard Mustang, Camaro and other "youthmobiles," Cougar certainly qualified as well-equipped. Besides the standard hidden headlamps (with vacuum-operated doors) and sequential turn signals, there were the nicely trimmed and padded dash, bucket seats (a full-width bench with center armrest was optional), "deep-loop" floor carpeting, three-spoke steering wheel with "walnut grain texture," floor shifts for all transmissions plus subtle exterior pinstriping (and surprisingly little chrome).

On the safety front were dual brake systems with a warning light, deluxe front and rear seatbelts with front retractors and a reminder light, safety padding on the dash, visors, A-pillars and steering hub, a new energy-absorbing steering column, safety door latches and locks, remote-control outside mirror, day/night center mirror on a breakaway arm, thick laminate safety-glass windshield, two-speed windshield wipers with washers, four-way emergency flasher and more. Granted, most of this was federally mandated, but the Cougar team did go a few steps farther than required . . . and made the car nicer and easier to live with.

Sixteen exterior colors, plus various two-tone combinations and a choice of white or black vinyl top for those who liked such things, were available. Major features on the option list included power steering, power brakes (with or without front discs), cruise control, air conditioning, "sports" console and a dash-mounted AM radio/8-track stereo

tape sound system. Also available was a trick swing-away tilt steering wheel that moved to the side for easier entry or exit then swung back into place at its original tilt setting.

Popular price? Check. The standard Cougar coupe wore a $2851 sticker on its window, just $350 higher than the base '67 Mustang.

Responsive performance, rivaling the "best of the European road cars"? Hmmm. Magazine tests pegged the GT's 0–60 acceleration in the mid-to-high-7-second range and quarter-mile performance at just under 16 seconds and 90 mph—more than adequate by '67 ponycar standards and certainly faster than almost any affordable European coupe or sedan.

But handling was another story. Not that the Cougar was bad for its time; it wasn't. It rode somewhat less stiffly than the comparable Mustang or Camaro and therefore cornered less fiercely. But all three were still slow and heavy-feeling, even clumsy, by contemporary European standards simply because chassis sophistication was not yet an acquired skill (or a high priority) in Detroit.

The automotive press generally greeted the new sporty Mercury with enthusiasm, most writers referring to it as a "Mustang with class," or words to that effect—which, of course, it was. *Motor Trend* magazine was most impressed of all, naming Cougar its 1967 "Car of the Year" over the Camaro, Thunderbird, Eldorado and some other pretty formidable competition.

Because L-M couldn't build enough Cougars to have one in every dealership by introduction day, it decided instead to give Principal Motors in affluent Monterey, California (Mercedes and Jaguar country), a virtually unlimited supply for the first few weeks as a sort of marketing test. This interesting but questionable plan must have miffed other L-M dealers no end, but Principal did sell 29 of its first 30 Cougars in the first month. Similarly enthusiastic sales receptions soon followed the car across the nation, once dealers had some stock to sell.

The Cougar launch brought with it what would become one of the most enduring and widely recognized advertising symbols of all time: Chauncey the Cougar. Recruited from a California animal farm, Chauncey would perch regally on, in and near Cougar cars (and later on the Lincoln-Mercury sign, the "Sign of the Cat")—often growling ferociously, upstaging the likes of Cheryl Tiegs, Farrah Fawcett and Rachel Ward, all of whom appeared in Cougar ads early in their careers. Interesting, too, is the fact that the Cougar appealed immediately to a large number of women who bought it despite the fact that it (and other Mercurys) were promoted as "the Man's Car" for 1967.

Partly to keep things simple at the plant, and largely because there was not enough tooling money, the '67 Cougars arrived on the ponycar market with only one hardtop coupe body style. There was no convertible, no fastback. Mid-year, however, a couple of interesting new models appeared. The first, announced on January 9 and available in early February 1967, was the decidedly more luxurious and well-equipped XR-7. The second was the Dan Gurney Special, more obscure and much less significant (except, perhaps, from the collector's—or Gurney fan's— standpoint).

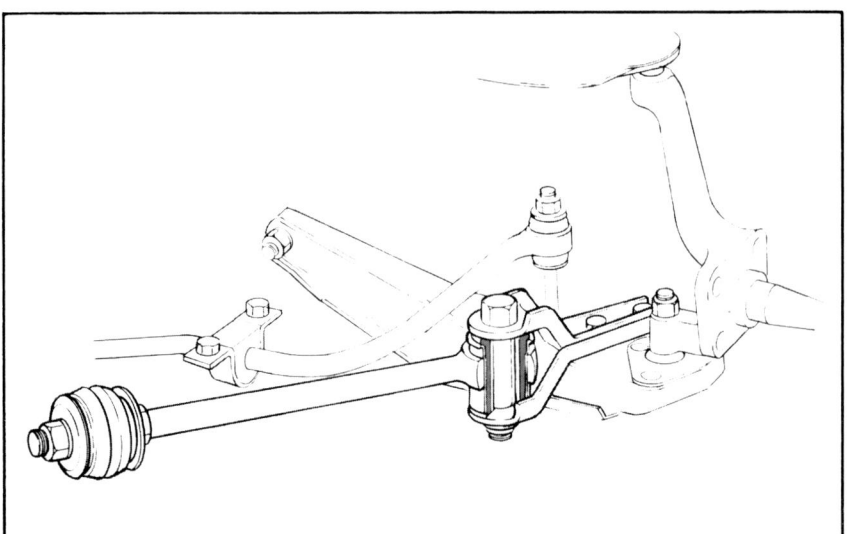

*Above: Cougar's articulated drag strut permitted better ride and handling. Left: A Cougar follows a Mustang coupe down the assembly line at Ford's Dearborn assembly plant. Right: The 1967 Cougar as seen beneath the skin*

The XR-7 carried the Cougar's Euro-interior theme a significant step further. Replacing the fuel gauge and warning lights in the right-hand instrument pod was a 6000-rpm tachometer, while spread across the upper dash were serious-looking round dials for fuel, temperature, oil pressure and battery discharge. The clock was relocated to a position under the radio in the standard vertical console. Above the center vent was a row of Jaguar-like toggle switches for the various map and courtesy lights, and above the center mirror was a futuristic (for 1967) overhead console containing both warning and map lamps. A burled walnut-look appliqué stretched wall-to-wall across the panel and "glove-soft" leather and vinyl upholstery covered the premium bucket seats. List price was $3081.41.

"We took the interior of the gran turismo car," said L-M General Manager and Ford Vice President E. F. (Gar) Laux at the XR-7's introduction, "which was formerly the exclusive possession of privileged classes in Europe and a comparative handful of affluent Americans, and while actually enhancing its utility, are making it available for a far lower cost than in its original form." Huh?

"In a nutshell," Laux clarified, "the Cougar XR-7 is the car for the man who aspires to an Aston Martin, but doesn't have James Bond's pocketbook." Oh.

The '67 Gurney Special was a low-volume spin-off of the XR-7 created to commemorate the famous racing star's role as captain of Mercury's powerful new SCCA Trans Am road-racing team. "Requests came down

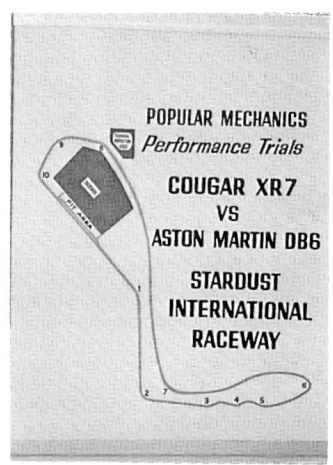

*Above: Popular Mechanics tested a 1967 XR-7 against an Aston Martin DB-6. Left: 1967 "Dan Gurney" Cougar was the basis for the 1968 GT-E.*

to do a Gurney special edition," former Cougar Design Manager John Aiken recalls, "and what we came up with was basically a two-tone paint scheme with badging. It was a beautiful maroon over a silver lower body." The two-tone paint scheme didn't make production—yet. But the package added an underhood chrome dress-up kit, special "turbine" wheelcovers and a Gurney signature decal on the rear-quarter window ... and little more. It was definitely *not* a high-performance model and should not be confused with the '68 GT-E. And no one seems to know how many were built.

Three months into the model year, more than 28,000 Cougars had been sold. That placed it third behind Mustang and Camaro among 11 U.S. "specialty" cars and actually ahead of Camaro on a per-dealer basis. While much of the industry was in a mild slump, Cougar sales continued to climb, and the plant was working overtime to meet demand. As soon as the first XR-7's hit the dealers' lots, they began accounting for 10 percent of Cougar sales and fully half of retail orders.

The 50,000th Cougar was sold on March 23, less than six months after the first. The XR-7 accounted for 20 percent of sales at that time and 40 percent of orders. L-M dealership floor traffic was up significantly as a result of the Cougar, according to Laux, and Mercury sales in general were stronger than the industry average because of, in his words, "... a transfer of some of the Cougar fun and excitement to the entire Mercury line." Much to Mercury's delight, more than half of the trades on new Cougars were competitive-make cars. When the 100,000 mark was passed in mid-July, Laux predicted 142,000 for the 1967 calendar year. He also announced that a second plant in San Jose, California, would be turning out Cougars in time for the '68 model year. In all, a total of 150,893 '67 Cougars were produced (of which 27,221 were XR-7's)

and model-year (October through September) sales hit 128,000.

On the SCCA's Trans Am racing circuit, the Gurney Cougar team scored a total of four wins (two by Formula One pilot Peter Revson, one each by Gurney and NASCAR ace David Pearson) and five second-place finishes, barely losing the season championship to in-house rival Ford with 62 points to Mustang's 64. The up-and-coming Penske Camaro team with driver Mark Donohue finished third in points with 57.

Nineteen sixty-eight brought minimal change to the successful Cougar package, except for the hot new GT-E model and a confusing proliferation of powertrains. The base powerplant was a new 302-cubic-inch two-barrel V-8 good for 210 horsepower on regular fuel. An optional higher-compression, four-barrel version gave 20 more horses on premium gas, while two- and four-barrel "Marauder" 390-cubic-inch V-8's offered 280 and 325 horsepower, respectively. A hairy 427-cubic-inch big-block rated at 390 horsepower came only in the GT-E, and only with Select-Shift Merc-O-Matic. All other engines were available with three-speed manual, four-speed manual or three-speed automatic—except the 390 two-barrel, which was automatic only. To confuse matters further, later in the year the 289 regular-gas V-8 reappeared with 195 horsepower in the base car, a 428 four-barrel conservatively rated at 335 horsepower was added, and the 390 four-barrel was redesignated "390 GT" with no apparent change in horsepower.

The GT-E boasted two-tone paint with a medium-silver lower body, (the color scheme proposed for the '67 Gurney) a "super competition handling package" (stiffer springs, adjustable heavy-duty shocks, bigger front swaybar), quad trumpet exhausts, "wide-tread" tires and a non-functional "power dome" on its hood. It also had its grille and tail lamp blades blackened out and two slim horizontal chrome strips across its face, and it could be equipped with either the base or the high-luxe XR-7 interior. Because it could not be built with a four-speed manual transmission, it was good for "only" about 7 seconds 0–60 and 15 seconds at 94 mph in the quarter-mile.

The '68 model also brought side marker lights and other new safety equipment, plus emissions-control air injection on manual-shift and high-compression 390 and 427 automatic models, in accordance with federal requirements. Lower-back-pressure inline exhaust systems replaced the former transverse type, and impact harshness at the front wheels was further softened through a new curved control arm strut with softer rubber bushings. New options for the year included front-seat headrests, a blower-type rear window defogger and a collapsible space-saver spare tire. List prices rose slightly to $2910 base, $3209 XR-7, $3313 GT and $4221 GT-E.

A limited-production Dan Gurney XR-7 version was again introduced in the spring. Designated XR7-G (yes, the hyphen officially moved), it featured a nonfunctional fiberglass hood scoop, fog lamps, "competition" hood pins, "racing" mirror, "European-type" chromed exhaust ports in the rear lower valence, wide-oval *radial* tires on unique spoke-pattern

**1968 Cougar XR-7 GT-E 427, owned by Gary L. Spear**

styled wheels, a special "sports" console, real walnut shift knob, simulated leather-wrapped steering wheel and a new power sunroof, the latter also offered on other Cougar models. Between 300 and 400 '68 XR7-G's were built, but the exact number remains unknown.

The exact number of GT-E's produced that year *is* known and it was a pretty sad showing. Just 358 were built with the 427 engine, then 244 more with the less expensive 335-horse 428 "Cobra Jet" V-8 that replaced the 427 in early April. This new top-of-the-line performance engine was available in any Cougar model with either four-speed manual or three-speed automatic, and it came with functional "Ram Air" hood scoop, a high-torque "Traction-Lok" differential, heavy-duty brakes and battery and the "competition" handling package.

Results on the racing circuits were mixed for the 1968 season. On one hand, the corporation disbanded Gurney's factory Trans Am team to concentrate on a repeat championship for Ford Division's Mustang—only to see the Penske/Donohue Camaro Juggernaut roll over both the Mustang team and the few independents still running Cougars. On the other hand, oval-track star Tiny Lund used one of the '67 Trans Am Cougars to capture nine wins and the driver's championship in NASCAR's fledgling Grand Touring Class. Lloyd Ruby and David Pearson, also Cougar drivers, won one event apiece, resulting in a total of 11 victories in 19 events and a manufacturer's championship for Mercury. There was also a successful factory-backed NHRA "Funny Car" drag-racing effort headed by "Dyno" Don Nicholson, who set several world

**Left: Drivers Dan Gurney, Ed Leslie and Parnelli Jones were the first members of Team Cougar. Above: Jones tests Cougar at Virginia International Raceway.**

records and became a feature attraction wherever he went.

Unfortunately, Cougar sales slid to about 110,000 and production to 113,726 for model-year '68. Exactly 32,712 of those were XR-7's.

John Aiken supervised the styling of a new-look Cougar for 1969, which he admits did not come off as well as his '67-'68. "Looking back on it now," he says, "the first effort was the better one. The '69 got bigger, puffier and a little heavier-looking." The trademark hidden headlamps and sequential turn signals were retained, but gone was the distinctive vertical-blade "electric shaver" look, replaced by a horizontal-rib motif in front. What had been the body-color nose was now just a bulge in the grille, and an awkward Buickesque character line plunged down the side from front fender to rear wheel.

Not only did the 1969 Cougar *look* longer and wider, it was—by 3.5 and 2.9 inches, respectively. The good news for fans of comfort and luxury was that the new interior was roomier and plusher. The best news for open-air motoring buffs was the first offering of a Cougar convertible, complete with a trick top framework design that let the rag roof fold down nearly flush with the fenders. The system also included a hidden-

*Above: Mustang versus Cougar at Daytona 300 in February 1967. Below and right: Team Cougar won one-two at Riverside's Mission Bell 250 in September 1967.*

**1969 Cougar Convertible, owned by Herm and Gay Sterner**

hinge glass rear window that folded in two when the top was down.

The standard engine for '69 was a two-barrel, 250-horsepower, regular-gas 351 V-8, but a four-barrel premium-fuel option offered 40 horsepower more. Also available were the 320 horsepower 390 four-barrel and the 335 horsepower 428 Cobra Jet, the latter with a choice of conventional or Ram Air induction. Three-speed manual came standard with both 351's, while four-speed manual or automatic could be ordered with any Cougar engine. The torque-sensitive Traction-Lok rear end was also offered with any engine, as was the competition-handling suspension—which now included staggered rear shocks to resist spring wind-up and wheel-hop during those rush-hour full-throttle burnouts. New on the option list were power windows, dual door-mounted stereo speakers and a "rim-blow" steering wheel whose horn pad was a continuous strip on the back surface of its circumference. Prices swelled once again to $3016 base, $3315 XR-7, $3382 convertible and $3595 XR-7 convertible.

The slow-selling GT-E was dropped, but the spring of 1969 brought a special new high-performance Cougar. In an obvious reference to drag racing (which seems not too astute given the upscale audience L-M intended for the Cougar), it was called the Cougar Eliminator, and it came with the regular choice of standard 351 or optional 428 CJ V-8, with or without Ram Air, or a high-revving "Boss" 302 V-8 straight from the

Boss 302 Mustang. The Boss was Ford's homologation special for SCCA Trans Am and amateur road racing as well as the answer to Chevy's Camaro Z-28.

This mighty-mite small-block featured huge canted valves in "semi-hemi" tunnel-port heads, an aluminum intake manifold with individual runners, forged-aluminum "pop-up" pistons, forged-steel rods, a cross-drilled forged-steel crankshaft, header-type free-flow exhaust manifolds, a high-lift, high-overlap cam, solid lifters and just about everything else in Ford's racing book. It was rated a laughably conservative 290 horsepower in street trim. At the Eliminator's announcement at the Chicago Auto Show in March, a beefy NASCAR-type 429 specifically for Super Stock drag racing was also promised, but there was no mention of that monster-motor at the car's actual introduction two months later. If any 429's did find their way into '69 Cougars, they must have been sold under the proverbial table.

Oh yes, the Eliminator was distinguished by newly fashionable front and rear spoilers, blacked-out grille, argent styled-steel wheels, flatback hood scoop, a black "performance" strip along its beltline and "Eliminator" identification in big block letters on its flanks; inside were high-back

1969 Cougar Eliminator Boss 302, owned by Bud Pennington

*Below: "Dyno" Don Nicholson's 1500-horsepower 427 sohc-powered Cougar Eliminator "funny car" was campaigned in 1968 NHRA events.*

bucket seats with integral headrests and a "rally" clock and tachometer. Power front disc brakes, F-70x14 bias-belted tires and a choice of wide- or close-ratio four-speed manual transmissions were also part of the deal, the first with a 3.91:1 rear axle, the other with a 4.30:1 axle for serious drag competition. The four available colors were white, bright blue metallic, competition orange and bright yellow. Interestingly, the Eliminator was not a separate model but an option package modestly priced (it included no special engine, remember) at just $130. A second $70 "Eliminator Decor Group" primarily added convenience equipment and more luxurious trim.

**Left: The Cougar GT-E was offered only in 1968. Below: Dan Gurney with the prototype for the second Cougar bearing his name, the 1968 XR7-G**

**1969 Cougar Eliminator 428 Super Cobra Jet, owned by John P. Karleskind Jr.**

*Above and below: Pre-production prototype for 1969 Cougar Eliminator; note non-production wheels and rear spoiler.*

*Above: Ford's potent Boss 302 was first offered as an option in 1969. Below: Rupp's Super Sno-Sport snowmobile poses alongside 1969 Cougar coupe.*

*Above: Dana-Spicer two-speed "Streeper" rear axle was considered for 1969. Below: 1970 Cougar Eliminator alongside "Super" Cobra Jet 428 V-8.*

How fast were these cars? With the Ram Air "Super" Cobra Jet 428, rumored to produce well over 400 horsepower despite its 335 horsepower rating, drag-prepared Eliminators were good for sub-14-second quarter-miles at 104 mph. With the road-racing-oriented 302, quarter-miles were still under 15 seconds and over 98 mph.

Thanks to safety and emissions requirements, and sky-high insurance rates, ponycar sales in general were slipping, and the musclecar's days were numbered as the turbulent Sixties neared their end. Cougar sales fell below 100,000 for the first time in model year '69, and production numbered just over that mark at 100,069. Of those, 23,918 were XR-7 coupes, 4024 were XR-7 convertibles and 5796 were standard convertibles. The '69 Eliminator package sold somewhat better than the costly '68 GT-E model had, with 2411 delivered.

When the '70 Mercurys debuted in the fall of 1969, the Cougar displayed only minor cosmetic and equipment changes. The vertical-bar grille and tail lamps were back, the former divided again by a protruding sheetmetal nose, with a bold insert matching the grille texture. High-back bucket seats became standard, while powertrains were again reshuffled as the engineers tried to satisfy the performance demands of the marketplace and the government's emissions requirements all at once. A regu-

**1970 Cougar Eliminator Boss 302, owned by Randy Marble**

lar-fuel 250-horsepower 351 two-barrel was standard, with a brand-new 300-horsepower four-barrel 351 Cleveland engine (with canted valves similar to the Boss 302's) optional in everyday Cougars and standard with the Eliminator package. Other engine options included the 290-horsepower Boss 302, the 335-horsepower 428 CJ and Ram Air "Super" CJ and a tamed-down version of the NASCAR 429 called "Boss 429," with normal heads and a 375-horsepower rating. A high-performance Hurst shifter came standard with all four-speed manual Cougars. Prices were $3114 base, $3413 XR-7, $3480 convertible,

**Styling prototype for 1970 Eliminator.**

$3692 XR-7 convertible.

Cougar production fell to only 72,363 for the '70 model year, 18,565 of which were XR-7 coupes. Of the 4299 convertibles built, 1977 were XR-7's. And the Eliminator—last of the true musclecar Cougars—sold to the tune of just 2200.

The Mustang grew again for '71, and therefore so did the Cougar. Its wheelbase stretched to 112.1 inches; its overall length to 196.7 inches, its width to 75.1 inches and front and rear treads to 61.5 and 61.0 inches, respectively. Mercury's once-small specialty car was now more a luxury intermediate than a performance-image ponycar, both in size and character. The shape was a bit more porky, the look (with the quad headlamps fully exposed for the first time) a bit more mainstream, and the interior and ride were definitely more cushy. *Motor Trend* called the '71 Cougar " . . . a car in search of an identity." Lincoln-Mercury called it the " . . . most completely equipped specialty sports car." And, while the '71 Cougar could still be ordered with some pretty exciting hardware, those two comments pretty well summed it up.

Available engines included the regular-gas two-barrel 351—slightly detuned to 240 horsepower—the four-barrel 351 rated at 285 horsepower, and a fairly hot, high-compression (11.3:1) "CJ" 429 rated at 370 horsepower with or without Ram Air. There was also a new low-compression (9.0:1) 351 CJ with a 285-horsepower rating, apparently intended for either regular or low-octane unleaded fuel. The "GT" label was revived to replace the discontinued Eliminator, and (like the Eliminator option) it was attached to an option package available only on the coupe. New "flow-thru" ventilation and a center "consolette" became standard in all Cougars, while side door beams and other safety equipment were added to satisfy Federal laws. Prices were $3289 base, $3629 XR-7, $3681 convertible and $3877 XR-7 convertible.

Standard Cougar production for 1971 totaled 34,008 coupes and 1723 convertibles, while XR-7's out the factory door numbered 25,416 coupes and 1717 ragtops. Grand total: a disappointing 62,864, only 723 of which were equipped with the GT package.

Nineteen seventy-two brought little cosmetic or equipment change and bad powertrain news as all engines except that a trio of low-compression (8.6:1), unleaded-fuel 351's were dropped, due to tough emissions standards. The base offering was a two-barrel version giving 164 horsepower under the newly adopted (and more realistic) SAE net rating system; it was available with a choice of three-speed manual or three-speed automatic. Optional were two four-barrel editions: the first rated at 262 horsepower with automatic only, the second (part of a "CJ Performance Group" that also included dual exhausts) at 266 horsepower with either automatic or four-speed manual. Sticker prices were actually *down* for '72 at $3061 base, $3323 XR-7, $3370 convertible and $3547 XR-7 convertible. Production was a dismal 53,702, of which 26,802 were XR-7 coupes, 1240 were base convertibles and 1929 XR-7 convertibles.

**1971 Cougar XR-7, owned by Ford Motor Company**

Then it was 1973, a watershed year for the auto industry. First came the heavy and often ugly 5-mph front bumpers, then record sales and optimism followed by the OPEC oil embargo and fuel crisis—all leading, as the year ground to a close, to a massive realignment of consumer values and manufacturer priorities—plus a new ration of federal laws mandating corporate average fuel economy. The Cougar—like every car sold in the United States—got caught in the tumult.

Except for the 5-mph bumper, and the 3 inches and 100-plus pounds it added, the '73 Cougar was virtually unchanged from the '72. Its available engines numbered only two: a two-barrel 351 rated at 168 horsepower

**1972 Cougar XR-7, owned by Robert A. Wool**

*L-M chief William P. Benton (right) with the last Cougar convertible.*

and a four-barrel version producing 264. Both came with three-speed automatic transmission as standard equipment; only the latter offered a four-speed manual option. Prices rose slightly to $3372 base, $3679 XR-7, $3726 convertible and $3903 XR-7 convertible. And, riding the coattails of the great sales year enjoyed by the industry as a whole, so did production. The total: 60,628. More than half, 35,110, were XR-7's; 4449 were ragtops, a fairly impressive 3165 of which were top-of-the-line XR-7 models. This was also the last year there would be an open-air Cougar, and a fair number of potential collectors knew it.

In 1973, however, the Cougar was facing the first of several major redefinitions. As a spinoff of the higher-volume Mustang, of course, it was always at the mercy of the rival Ford Division's plans; bigger, heavier, more powerful engines intended to win buyers by winning races inevitably led to bigger, fatter and heavier cars that turned away those same potential buyers. Eventually, the original, successful concept of the small, agile ponycar was lost. And you can blame the usual enemies as well: excessive government regulation, insurance company avarice, the fuel crisis.

The most plausible answer was that the Cougar, after its first couple of happy years, didn't really know what kind of cat it wanted to be. Was it a feline Mustang . . . a land-bound, four-legged 'Bird . . . an all-American Jaguar? Was it a luxury coupe . . . a road racer . . . a *drag* racer? After a while, it was trying to be all of those and more to all sorts of buyers, and no one at Lincoln-Mercury seemed to know in which direction to more precisely aim it.

**1973 Cougar XR-7, owned by Robert J. Hahn**

# PART TWO: IN SEARCH OF AN IMAGE, 1974-1982

Even in the late Sixties, well before the Arab Oil Embargo and the resulting fuel shortage of 1973-74, members of Motor City boardrooms were gradually reaching a collective conclusion that the industry's delightfully irresponsible musclecar wars could not be sustained much longer. Ever-tightening emissions standards were strangling the big-inch engines, while inflating insurance tariffs were choking their owners' budgets. Escalating safety requirements added cost and weight, while safety advocates leveled stinging criticism at Detroit's automakers and lobbied for increasingly stringent legislation.

One key consideration among Ford Motor Company managers, therefore, was what to do with their pair of already oversize and overweight ponycars, the Mustang and Cougar. With public enthusiasm for such cars on the wane and their shared unibody platform becoming less profitable as its volume declined, some advocated dropping them entirely. Others argued for their continuation despite the cost of redesigning them, accurately citing the need for youthful, sporty image-leaders for both Ford and Lincoln-Mercury divisions.

A third proposal (which must have seemed brilliant at the time) was to retain both and send them in different directions. Ford's Mustang would become much smaller, lighter and more affordable for younger buyers on tighter budgets. It would even offer a frugal four-cylinder engine. Mercury's Cougar, meanwhile, would move upscale in size, opulence and price to do battle with General Motors' successful mid-size "personal" coupes: the Chevrolet Monte Carlo, Pontiac Grand Prix, Oldsmobile Cutlass and Buick Century.

In the process, each would be integrated into existing car families—Mustang built on the subcompact Pinto platform, and the Cougar on the all-new, body-on-frame intermediate platform then being developed for a '72 introduction. This kept both famous names in their respective stables while saving great gobs of tooling and development dollars. It coincided with a potentially profitable philosophy of offering specialty coupes for a full spectrum of buyers and budgets, with the Lincoln Mark at the top and what would become the new baby Mustang at the bottom.

Finally, this plan would install the proposed larger, plusher Cougar in the slot once occupied by Ford Division's flagship Thunderbird, which itself had migrated well upscale since its '58-model stretch to four-seat status. The company's plan for the formerly sporty T-Bird, in fact, had it moving even further upward onto a stetched "luxury" version of this same new mid-size chassis—along with what would be the '72 Lincoln Mark IV.

It all made perfect sense, both strategically and financially. And that's why it ultimately happened exactly that way.

"When we did the new intermediates for '72," recalls Howard Freers, the engineer responsible for that program, "the Thunderbird and Mark became derivatives with a lengthened wheelbase and some beefing up of the suspension. I had been Chief Engineer-Light Cars, but then they dreamed up the title 'Chief Engineer-Light and Luxury Cars' because we brought in those luxury coupes." The near-twin intermediate-size members of that family became the Ford Torino and Mercury Montego.

Like Torinos, mid-size Montegos came in coupe, sedan and wagon variations. They were nice enough cars for their time, adequately filling the gap between the full-size Mercury Marquis and the compact Comet. The last of the ponycar Cougars, meanwhile, was living out its life in the face of accelerating government regulation, declining performance and decreasing buyer interest. By the end of 1973, the year that brought both battering-ram bumpers and crisis-born fuel-consciousness to the American industry, the ponycar Cougar was gone.

And in its place when the '74 models made their debut that fall was a new and different breed of Cougar. There was only one model, the XR-7, and it was essentially a plusher Montego coupe embellished with Mark IV styling cues—chromed radiator shell, thrusting "bladed" front fenders, a padded "landau" roof and even Mark-like "opera" windows—all of which helped position it as a mini-Mark for those who aspired to the Lincoln's image but lacked the requisite resources.

"That program was kind of tough for us," explains Executive Designer Gail Halderman, who headed Lincoln-Mercury Design at the time. "It was difficult trying to do what we thought of as a small specialty car on that big platform . . . until we hit upon the idea of making it the 'poor man's Mark.' That got us thinking totally differently, and I think it made it work somewhat. That's also how we sold it to [then Ford Vice President] Iacocca. He called it his blue-collar-workers' Mark.

"We were still trying to do a lot of it with mirrors. We did things with front ends, decklids and hoods. You know Iacocca—he liked vertical grilles, and they had to be 28½ inches wide; they had to be dominant; they had to have an ornament on top. He also liked bladed fenders; 'I want the reach,' he said. He wanted things to happen, wanted this car to be visually exciting in every view—front end, rear end, side view."

It was the combination of those cues that set the '74 XR-7 apart from the ordinary Montego (or, for that matter, the Ford Torino) coupe. In engineering terms, Freers confirms that it was essentially identical to a two-door Torino. "It was a decent-looking automobile, but character-wise—suspension, handling—I don't remember any difference at all. It was just the different skin and whatever trim differences we put on it."

It may have been a "new appearance, new dimensions, new construction and a new marketing stance," as the introductory press release stated, but the new Cougar's standard equipment list was familiar: 351-

*Cougar production moved to Atlanta, Georgia, starting with 1974 model year.*

cubic-inch V-8, automatic "SelectShift" transmission, power (front disc, rear drum) brakes, power steering, full instrumentation and HR78x14 steel-belted radial tires. Also standard was the ill-conceived seatbelt/ignition interlock system that prevented the car from being started until front occupants were buckled up. Most buyers quickly found a way to disable it, and Congress soon rescinded the National Highway Transportation Safety Administration standard that required it.

The base 351 engine was really two different engines of equal displacement and similar performance, both fed through two-barrel carburetors. Most '74 Cougars got the 162-horsepower "Windsor" 351, while California cars and some others were fitted with 163-horsepower "Cleveland" units. Optional choices included a 170-horsepower two-barrel 400-cubic-inch V-8, a 220-horsepower four-barrel 460, and (except in California, where emissions standards were tougher) a high-performance four-barrel 351 rated at 255 horsepower. Ford's new solid-state ignition was standard on the two larger powerplants and on

*Trainers Pat and Ted Derby with their Cougars, Chauncey and Christopher.*

all engines equipped for California emissions.

In accordance with standard Ford design practice of the time, noise, vibration and harshness (NVH) treatment was extensive. The body, for example, sat on tuned mounts that permitted some flexing of the frame on rough roads with minimal disturbance to the passenger compartment. The suspension was also standard Ford: upper and lower control arms with fore-aft compliance struts, tube shocks inside coil springs, and a stabilizer bar in front; four-link, live axle with coil springs and angled shocks in back. A heavy-duty Cross-Country suspension option added stiffer springs, tougher shocks, a rear stabilizer bar and a heavier front bar.

The big Cougar's styling began with fashionable long-hood/short deck coupe proportions and finished with the Lincoln Mark-like ornamentation. Its front windshield pillars were thin and set at a rakish (by 1974 standards at least), 55 degrees. The little portholes in the wide rear C-pillars were similar to the Mark IV's elegant ovals. "Iacocca wanted the Mark identification," says Halderman. "But he didn't want to copy that oval. So we took the oval and angled off the ends in a straight line." A band of argent around the periphery framed the etched metal Cougar emblem laminated inside its glass.

The grille up front was a slightly smaller and more rounded version of the Mark IV's squared-off, Rolls-Royce-reminiscent shell. The face it dominated was much like the '73 Cougar's, with the grille's vertical texture repeated in deep-set horizontal side grilles framing dual headlamps on either side and extending to large parking lamps in the fenders' leading edges. In back, wraparound horizontal tail lamps connected by a center reflector gave a full-width look, with bright vertical bars repeating the front grille theme. The 16.5-cubic-foot trunk was a 37 percent improvement over the '73's cargo capacity.

The '74 Cougar's plush cabin came with either bucket seats or a Mark IV-style "Twin Comfort Lounge" split bench. Between the buckets was a console incorporating the gear selector and a covered stowage box/armrest, while the split bench featured twin fold-down armrests. Soft expanded vinyl upholstery in a wide vertical pleat design was standard, a choice of luxury cloth or a vinyl/leather combination optional. The new instrument panel featured three large, round pods to the left and five smaller ones to the right. The big ones contained an adjustable air register, a 6000-rpm tachometer and a circular speedometer complete with trip odometer. The smaller pods housed fuel, temperature, battery and oil pressure gauges and a clock, all angled toward the driver.

Despite a near-depression year for the U.S. industry in general, 1974 proved the new, larger Cougar a stroke of marketing magic. While total Lincoln-Mercury sales fell by more than 100,000 units, or 20 percent, Cougar sales for the model year improved by nearly 50 percent over 1973 to nearly 79,000. Ponycar purists and owners of earlier Cougars may have been unhappy with the change, but the public in general seemed eager to embrace the mini-Mark idea.

Helping promote the "new" Cougar was none other than Chauncey the

*Left: 1974 Cougar XR-7, owned by Ford Motor Company. Above: 1975 Cougar XR-7, owned by Ford Motor Company.*

Cougar, the snarling cat who became a legendary trademark for Cougar and Lincoln-Mercury in general. As part of a fundraising effort for the Fund for Animals and Love is an Animal, Lincoln-Mercury sponsored a cross-country trip in the fall of 1973 for Chauncey; his owners, Ted and Pat Derby; his cohort, two-year old Christopher the Comet; and a white 1974 XR-7 autographed by over 100 celebrities. Not surprisingly, Chauncey and Christopher were popular attractions: "We had 10,300 people visit our dealership the day Chauncey appeared," said Paul Steitzer of Steitzer Lincoln-Mercury in Cedar Rapids, Iowa. "Cars were backed up for miles. . . . I've never seen anything like it."

At the time, Chauncey was the veteran of six years in front of the camera as the Cougar's mascot, and was so well trained that he would issue his trademark snarl with a hand command from Ted Derby. Unfortunately, Chauncey's snarl was silenced in August of the following year, when he died of old age. His place was taken by young Christopher, who remained the Cougar mascot until 1979.

The 1975 XR-7 was little changed except for the addition of a power moonroof (like the Mark IV's it was one-way tinted glass with a manually-operated opaque shade) and other new options, including a Security Lock Group, a Space-Saver spare tire and a fuel-economy reminder light. Cooling slots were added to the front bumper beneath the grille, solid-state ignition became standard across the board, and the windshield washer nozzles were moved to the wiper arms. Sadly, the high-performance four-barrel 351 was dropped and the other engines were down from 3 to as much as 26 horsepower due to emissions-related modifications. A Cougar counterpart called Elite had been added to the Ford Torino stable in mid-'74, and sales surged to 118,000 units that year and 102,000 in calendar 1975. Cougar sales, however, slid to 49,200 from the previous year's level of nearly 80,000.

Nineteen seventy-six was another no-change year for Ford's mid-size cars as fuel-shortage fears moved to the back of America's minds and the industry began a strong recovery. "Cougar is the symbol of Lincoln-Mercury," Division General Manager and Ford Vice President Walter S. Walla declared at the September 3, 1975, press introduction. "And no car better embodies the spirit and theme of the division." To keep its base price down (and per-unit profit up), Walla's marketing men installed a cheaper "flight bench" seat and moved the Twin-Comfort-lounge and bucket seats to the option list, along with the previously standard tinted glass, luxury steering wheel and styled-steel wheels. The Cougar's full instrumentation survived, however, while power teams remained unchanged and optional cast-aluminum wheels were added. Sales improved significantly, reaching more than 80,000 units for the model year.

But if Cougar fans had been disappointed by the car's altered size and image in '74, they must have been shocked senseless when the wraps were pulled from the '77 models in the fall of 1976. Mercury's mid-size Montego series had been less than successful over the years, while the Cougar still basked in the image magic it had earned back in the late

**1976 Cougar XR-7, owned by Ford Motor Company**

Sixties. So Lincoln-Mercury managers did what any smart salesperson would do: They restyled the entire line, giving it a cleaner, crisper, less voluptuous look (resembling that of the new-for-'77 Lincoln Mark V) and spread the Cougar name all the way across it.

Thus Cougar XR-7 owners would be confronted with the specter of meeting workaday Cougar two-door hardtops, four-door sedans and even (gasp!) station wagons on the road and in their neighborhoods. From the perspective of an industry bouncing back from a painful recession, this move made perfect short-term sense. In the long term, thought, it would place the Cougar's image in serious jeopardy.

Designer Halderman recalls that the Montego "really had a problem because it had no identity at all. It didn't have a good name; it was nothing but Lincoln-Mercury's version of the Ford Torino—a 'me, too' kind of car—and it was struggling. It was a very vanilla car, and we didn't know what to do with it to make it different. Cougar at least had a heritage and a little more class."

Over at Ford Division, meanwhile, the Master Plan stipulated that the lumbering Mark-based Thunderbird would give way to a new and much less expensive mid-size Thunderbird, which replaced the Elite as Ford's Torino-based personal coupe. Then the Torino series name was changed to LTD II in hopes of luring former full-size Ford owners moving downward into something more efficient. And that is how the Cougar, once Mercury's Mustang counterpart, became the Thunderbird's badge-engineered cousin.

"It was a marketing strategy," Halderman continues, "and we didn't necessarily agree with it. Here at Design we were a little concerned that Cougar was losing its prestige and identity, and when you spread that out thinner and thinner, it's tough, real tough, to retain it. It was a bit of a struggle to do Cougar four-doors; and then, once we'd swallowed that,

**1977 Cougar XR-7, owned by Ford Motor Company**

they said, 'OK, now we want you to make a wagon.' That was strictly a mirror job, taking an existing wagon and plunking on the vertical grille texture and hood ornament."

Distinguishing the prestige XR-7 from everyday Cougars was a new rear roof design with larger opera windows partially covered by simulated louvers, plus exclusive wraparound tail lamps and a sculptured "spare tire" rear deck similar to the Mark V's. Halderman admits he was not overly pleased with that design: "That was a period of time when Iacocca and others would wander in and say, 'What can you guys do to this thing to make it unique and pull it further away from its counterparts at Ford Division? We need something unique, just a little something.' We'd say, 'We don't want to hoke this thing up.' But we ended up doing a lot of hoke-up jobs just trying to be different."

The Cougar Brougham sedan also sported C-pillar windows to set it apart from lesser four-doors and its LTD II cousins. "That one was a struggle," says Halderman, "because it didn't quite fit that C-pillar. There was structure where we wanted to put it, so it ended up being a real compromise. It was, again, trying to give that car some uniqueness, and it probably added something."

Division General Manager Walt Walla unveiled the '77 Cougars on September 7, 1976. "For the first time," he said, "the excitement and styling flair associated with Cougar in the past will be available in a family-sized car a cut above the ordinary intermediates. The Cougar XR-7 should be an even stronger entry in the intermediate specialty market where unique styling and luxury appointments play an important role. Cougar and Cougar Brougham models will offer first-class family transportation in a comfortable, six-passenger package."

A smaller and lighter 302-cubic-inch (5.0-liter) two-barrel V-8 rated at 130 horsepower replaced the 351 as base engine (except in station wagons), while the big 460 was deleted from the Cougar's option list. A 149-horsepower 351 Windsor V-8, a 161-horsepower "modified" version and a 173-horse 400 were optional choices—the latter two in California and high-altitude areas (which had different emissions requirements as well)—and all featured second-generation electronic ignition. Handling, meanwhile, was improved with the addition of standard 15-inch wheels and a rear stabilizer bar.

One interesting feature on '77 Cougars was a hinged grille that could swing inward to protect itself in minor impacts. The interior was also freshened with new instrument panel and door trim designs, plus an ultra-plush decor option available in Brougham and XR-7 models. Full "Sports" instrumentation, unfortunately, joined the option list along with such newly available goodies as AM/FM/MPX radio with a quadrasonic (remember that?) eight-track tape player and an Illuminated Entry System that activated both the interior lights and a lighted ring around the doorlock cylinder when either door handle was raised.

A September 30, 1977, press release compared the 1977 Cougar in terms of dollar value to the first 1967 Cougar introduced 10 years earlier. "If purchased with 1976 dollars," Walla pointed out, "a comparably equipped 1967 Cougar would have cost $1,514 more than a 1977 base Cougar two-door." (Note that he was comparing the $3,261 '67 model to the bottom-line $4,766 '77 hardtop, not the better-equipped $5,274 XR-7.) Walla added that while the '77 was 800 pounds heavier, it bettered the '67 in EPA fuel economy at 17 mpg (combined city/highway) compared to an estimated 15.8 for the '67. In addition, he said, the newest Cougar was much "cleaner" in exhaust emissions. It was smoother riding, quieter, safer, better-protected in terms of paint adhesion, rustproofing and damageability in minor impacts (due to its mandated 5-mph bumpers) and even more reliable thanks to solid-state ignition and better wiring systems.

Maybe so. But measured by other important criteria—handling, performance, sportiness and youthfulness—Cougar enthusiasts would counter that their car had departed a long way from the much-loved original of a decade before.

In its May, 1977 issue, *Car and Driver* called the XR-7 "a twin to Ford's new compact Thunderbird. Both have 114 inches between the wheels and measure 215 inches overall—dimensions that differ only fractionally from those of the Monte Carlo, Chrysler Cordoba, Dodge Charger and all of the other players in the intermediate specialty field." Engineering Editor Pat Bedard went on to label the Cougar as "undiluted Ford, particularly the way it rides and drives." Its optional 351 two-barrel, he said was "modest in its capabilities." But he praised the styling as "tautly drawn and crisply angled" and the interior, especially the fully-optioned instrument panel, as the design element ". . . that most pleases the eye." Bedard added that the expensive optional Moonroof was nice but soaked up a lot of headroom, and that the trunk wasn't much good for items larger than grocery bags. "But with the right options," he concluded, "the Cougar happily takes its place in the world of painless transportation." Faint praise, indeed.

Retail sales for the calendar year, however, seemed to vindicate the marketers' strategy by climbing to nearly 183,000 for Cougar as a whole and 130,000 for the XR-7 alone. The designers, engineers and faithful fans may have been distressed, but the sales department and L-M divisional managers wore ear-to-ear grins. "The Cougar nameplate has accounted for one of every four Lincoln-Mercury sales during the 1977 model year," boasted Walla as he introduced the '78s, "a record pace and one of the best performances by a single car line in division history."

Functional changes to the '78 Cougar line were limited to subtle aerodynamic improvements, lower-backpressure exhaust systems, a new lightweight power steering pump and a few other details. Styling was also unchanged except for the usual fiddling with paint and vinyl top colors. New options included a power antenna (XR-7 only), a 40-channel CB radio (with a remote-mounted chassis and detachable microphone) and a Midnight/Chamois Decor Group for the XR-7 that featured either blue or chamois exterior paint, a contrasting half-vinyl roof and decklid

*1979 Cougar Brougham Sedan, owned by Ford Motor Company*

appliqué, and a special blue cloth interior with chamois accents in a kinky belt-buckle motif.

The station wagon was dropped in preference to the new-for-'78 compact Zephyr wagon, which was smaller, lighter and more efficient yet could carry nearly as much cargo. That made the 13,095 '77 Cougar wagons built collector cars of sorts, though with questionable desirability. "My daughter has one that she advertised for sale," Halderman said, "and people called and said, 'A *Cougar* wagon? I didn't know they made one.' " Cougar sales for calendar 1978 (the third-best year in domestic U.S. history) totaled 195,000; nearly 160,000 were XR-7's.

For 1979, its 40th anniversary year, Mercury launched a brand-new full-size Marquis and a new-generation Capri (now a cousin to the all-new Mustang), while carrying over the Cougar series again with little change. "As the last of the traditional intermediate cars," said new Lincoln-Mercury General Manager and Ford Vice President Walter J. Oben, "we anticipate that the Cougars will increase their already exceptional customer acclaim in 1979." What he meant, roughly translated, was: "We sure hope the new smaller, lighter and more contemporary GM and

Chrysler downsized intermediates don't kill our Cougar sales this year."

There were new grille and tail lamp treatments, new chamois and velour cloth interiors for Decor Group XR-7s, and several new paint and trim colors. New to the option list were a long-range 27-gallon fuel tank and an AM/FM/cassette stereo radio (the latter a late-'78 addition). The 400-cubic-inch V-8 was dropped, leaving the standard (except in California) 302 rated at 133 horsepower and the optional 351) at 151 horsepower. All engines also got a new electronic voltage regulator and efficiency-enhancing carburetor modifications.

But 1979 began with the country's second fuel crisis (following the overthrow of the Shah of Iran) and closed with car sales and the economy in general headed for another deep recession. While the XR-7 remained high on the public's popularity list with calendar year sales over 121,000, the rest of the Cougar line suffered mightily as even loyal Mercury buyers opted for more efficient Monarchs and Zephyrs instead. Production of "ordinary" Cougars was halted, and the last of the 3,955 built that year were out the dealers' doors by August. Coincidentally, it was also August 1979 when Henry Ford II stepped down as Ford chairman, leaving the company that bears his name in the capable hands of Philip Caldwell, the first individual outside the Ford family ever to head it.

It was against that backdrop that Lincoln-Mercury Division would launch its least memorable and least successful new Cougar to date. As part of the overall downsizing scheme, both Thunderbird and Cougar were redone on the smaller, lighter Fairmont/Zephyr platform (which also made them relatives of the new Mustang and Capri introduced the previous year). In reality, both were little more than overdecorated Fairmont/Zephyrs, no longer seen by the public as cheaper alternatives to the elegant Lincoln Mark VI (which was also awkwardly shrunk) or even viable competitors to GM's successfully downsized specialty coupes.

Not that the '80 Thunderbird and Cougar were all that bad to drive. Properly optioned, they were crisper-handling, more enjoyable cars in almost every way (except ride and noise/harshness) than the bigger, heavier boats they replaced. Their acceptance problem seemed almost entirely a result of their schizophrenic styling, inside and out.

"It was one of those deals," says Halderman, "where we had to make the cars smaller, but management was afraid of the downsize. They said, 'Do everything you can to puff them up.' We tried to downsize without letting them *look* downsized, so we tried to compensate in squareness and height until the proportions got a little undesirable. We also took a lot of weight out but tried to make them not look like they'd been on a diet.

"I wish you could have seen the original theme model," he adds. "It was much, much better. It was a lot lower, had a lower-profile front fender and a lower deck, and it dropped off a little at the rear. And, through the execution of trying to get the car to look bigger and also trying to get it to package more efficiently, we raised the roof, raised the fenders, raised the hood, and we lost it. But you do this by spoonfuls, and you're so close to it that you really don't realize how bad it's getting. That's exactly what happened to that car."

Fuel efficiency was the topic of the day when General Manager Oben unveiled the 1980 Lincolns and Mercurys to the press on September 6, 1979. Boasting that the division's Corporate Average Fuel Economy (CAFE) was up from 19 mpg in 1979 to 20 for the 1980 model year (the average required by law), he pointed out that five L-M car lines would deliver 20 mpg or better on the combined city/highway driving cycle. They were: Bobcat, Capri and Zephyr at 28 mpg, Monarch at 22, and Cougar XR-7 at 20. All '80 Cougars were XR-7's, and he called their appearance "an exciting new variation of the popular styling theme. We believe we have improved on the Cougar XR-7's traditional excitement and sizzle in a highly efficient package that is in tune with the times. "Although its exterior will be smaller, Cougar XR-7 will retain all of the interior roominess, comfort and luxury

True enough. Although the 1980 Cougar was 15 inches shorter and 700 pounds lighter than its '79 counterpart, it offered virtually the same front seat room (for driver and one passenger), significantly *more* knee room and legroom for rear-seat occupants (thanks to a thinner front seat design) and a trunk larger by 2.0 cubic feet. Front suspension (as on Mustang/Capri and Fairmont/Zephyr) was strut-type with the coil spring

**A new 255-cubic-inch V-8 was added to Cougar lineup in 1980.**

*1980 Cougar XR-7, owned by Ford Motor Company*

*"Sports Group" option for 1980 included Recaro bucket seats.*

relocated inboard of the shock, while a conventional four-link, coil spring arrangement suspended the rear. Brakes remained front disc, rear drum with standard power assist, and steering was power rack-and-pinion.

Under the smaller XR-7's hood was either a brand-new smaller 255-cubic-inch (4.2-liter) standard V-8 or the old favorite 302 (5.0-liter). Standard transmission was a three-speed automatic, while the industry's first four-speed overdrive automatic was optionally available with the larger V-8 engine. California-bound Cougars also got EEC III, Ford's third-generation electronic engine control system. Other new functional features included sealed-beam halogen headlamps, low-rolling-resistance "P-metric" radial tires, "fluidic" windshield washers (emitting a single oscillating jet stream), a maintenance-free battery, and stalk-mounted controls for the headlamp dimmer, windshield wiper/washers and (controversially) the horn.

Four levels of XR-7—base, Decor Group, Luxury Group and Sports Group—were offered for 1980, the latter two including low-profile "TR-type" performance tires on cast-aluminum wheels. The Sports Group also featured its own two-tone paint treatment and a specially tuned handling suspension. Innovative new options—by Detroit standards, at least—included Recaro sport seats, a Keyless Entry System (five touch-sensitive numbered buttons on the outer door), and an electronic instrument panel (standard with the Luxury Group) with digital speedometer and graphic fuel level displays.

When *Motor Trend* tested a loaded Luxury Group XR-7 whose sticker price was a staggering $11,873 (nearly twice the Cougar's $6,569 base tariff), its observations were predictable: "The new vehicle hiding under all those extras is an improved personal luxury car," wrote then Executive Editor Jim McCraw in the March 1980 issue, "and the car is ineffably quiet inside, even when the road surfaces are ineffably bad outside."

Performance with the optional 5.0-liter engine (California-rated at 131 horsepower) was adequate—about 11 seconds 0–60 and 18 seconds at just over 75 mph in the quarter-mile. Measured fuel economy over *Motor Trend's* test loop was an impressive 23.5 mpg. But McCraw criticized the styling, inside and out, as unappealing and out of proportion. "The XR-7 was destined to be a derivative of the Thunderbird and has, therefore, been locked into a basic shape . . . [and] the items used to differentiate it from the Ford—the cat's-head emblem and the decklid bustle—do little to set its own image."

*1981 Cougar GS, owned by Ford Motor Company*

Spring 1980 brought what Oben called an "unprecedented" spring marketing program. "We are basing our campaign on pride," he said. But "desperation" might have been a more accurate word. The fact was, the industry's sales depression was its worst in modern times, and his cars just weren't moving. Cash rebates (an unfortunate last-ditch measure pioneered by Chrysler Corp. as it teetered on the brink of bankruptcy) were offered to buyers of both Zephyrs and XR-7's, while other Lincoln-Mercury models benefited from dealer incentives, financial assistance and supplemental advertising.

Ford's much cheaper (and somewhat less thirsty) 3.3-liter straight six was hurriedly prepared for XR-7 availability, and a variety of "special value packages" also helped move a few XR-7's off the lots. The combination of two-tone paint, luxury wheelcovers and wide door belt and bodyside moldings, for example, could be ordered at a retail savings of $147. Still, when all was said and done, Cougar XR-7 sales for model year 1980 totaled fewer than 70,000 units.

The marketers took charge again in 1981. First they added much of the former Decor Group's exterior ornamentation as standard. Then they shuffled the content of the remaining groups (making them mostly interior packages) and renamed them GS, LS and the "Recaro bucket seat option." Thus the prospective buyer could mix and match his or her choice of roof, tires and exterior features with the preferred level of interior opulence. Next they made the 3.3-liter straight six standard and both 4.2- and 5.0-liter V-8's optional, with or without the extra-cost overdrive automatic. Then they dropped the bomb: Replacing the aged Monarch as Mercury's mainstream mid-size entry was an upgraded Zephyr spinoff, available in both two-door and four-door sedan body styles and named (what else?) Cougar.

*Car and Driver* (June 1981) tested a Cougar sedan, called it "...a Fairmont not far under its skin" and conceded that it might fulfill its mission of snaring "fallen-away Mercury Marquis buyers who are looking for something a little more economical" because it "looks for all the world like a smaller version of the Marquis." Associate Editor Rich Ceppos contended, "The big-car illusion doesn't quite hold up once you're inside, however. In fact, our GS (middle trim level) test car could have been a well optioned Fairmont for all we knew." The two cars not only shared the same wheelbase and suspension, he said, but they also shared the same "homely" instrument panel.

Most disappointing, wrote Ceppos, was the car's handling, *despite* its handling-oriented TRX (Michelin) tire and suspension package. He asked a Lincoln-Mercury spokesperson why and was told, quite candidly, that the division had "no interest in selling responsive, road-hugging Cougars" and that "FoMoCo, in fact, had only one goal for the suspension: endowing the Fairmont pieces with 'big-car ride and isolation.'" Ceppos also noted that the 88-horsepower 3.3-liter six produced a lazy 14.3-second 0-60 time along with only "middling" fuel economy. "So what we have here, at best," he summarized, "is little more than an innocuous way for four or five people to get from place to place, an automobile that represents no significant improvement over the one it was based on."

In light of the staggering $1 *billion* a year losses the company was suffering even as this lackluster new car was introduced, Ceppos concluded, "We only hope Ford gets its crystal ball fixed soon." As we now know, Ford's crystal ball was in fact being nicely attended to by the new administration—President Donald Petersen, Design Vice President Donald Kopka and others—brought in by quiet but clear-visioned chairman Philip Caldwell. It wouldn't happen overnight; but it *was* happening.

Model year '82, however, brought more of the same limpid products. Still, new L-M general manager and Ford Vice President Gordon MacKenzie introduced his '82 lineup with a note of optimism: 1981 calendar-year sales for the division were up eight percent over the dismal figures of

*1982 Cougar Station Wagon, owned by Ford Motor Company*

1980. And two new models were added to the suffering division's stable: a Lynx five-door hatchback and (groan) a Cougar wagon.

"We listened carefully to the market on our mid-size cars, Zephyr, Cougar and XR-7," MacKenzie said. "The result is that we have upgraded product, emphasized value for money and offered special option packages.... We're taking a whole new approach to the XR-7 this year. There will be only one interior. Its twin-comfort lounge seat is covered with luxury velour cloth. In short, XR-7 has become a luxury car in a nonluxury price class.

"The Cougar line has added station wagon models for 1982," MacKenzie went on, "mid-size wagons that can carry six passengers in complete comfort, with cargo convenience. Cougar wagons have 74 cubic feet of cargo space. That's more than Chrysler K-cars or GM's mid-size wagons. Cougar's load floor is a full six and a half feet long with the back seat down."

'Nuff said? Well, not quite. There *was* a new, optional 112-horsepower, 3.8-liter V-6 engine, teamed with the four-speed overdrive automatic (the 5.0-liter V-8 was unceremoniously dropped) plus a lockup torque converter automatic for the 3.3-liter six. Base-trim Cougars were discontinued, leaving GS and LS levels; the XR-7's standard analog clock got new electronic workings, and an eight-function Tripminder trip computer was added to its option list. Other than trim and color changes and (for the sedan) a new deep-well trunk and an optional 20-gallon fuel tank, that was about it.

To the surprise of few, total model-year Cougar sales slid from 1981's 79,000 to about 67,000 units, of which roughly 34,000 in '81 and fewer than 18,000 in '82 were XR-7's. It was a sad but fitting end to an up and down era for a once-great car called Cougar.

## PART THREE: BUILDING A BETTER CAT, 1983-1987

New Ford Motor Company President Donald Petersen was credited by insiders and outsiders alike as a good "product man." He also had a "hands-off" management style, at least when it came to product programs. That combination was just what the corporate doctor ordered for recovery from the $1-billion-a-year slump Ford found itself in following the 1979 fuel crisis and the resulting economic recession. Such losses were not entirely *caused* by Ford's lack of good, competitive products for the Eighties, but they were exacerbated by it.

"We just had to get the basic thinking and implementing back in the hands of our professional people," Petersen explains. "I've always felt we had very talented professional people, yet we had gone astray because they hadn't really been in charge of doing their own things. There had been so many superimposed requirements, so many ideas about what sorts of things had to be accomplished, that bit by bit it had choked off their initiative and creativity. And so, part of what I tried to do was to encourage the technical people and the design people to go ahead and express what it was that they thought we ought to be doing."

Along those lines, Petersen had strode into the company's Design Center in June 1980, shortly after becoming president, to review a selection of proposed future products in clay and fiberglass. Among them was a theme model for the next-generation Thunderbird and Cougar, which he found—to put it mildly—underwhelming. "Would you be proud to have this car in your own driveway?" he asked Jack J. Telnack, then director of International, Special Vehicles and Advanced Concept Design. Telnack admitted that, no, he and his staff were not overly thrilled with the direction they had been pursuing under the previous administration. As he tells it: "He [Peterson] said, 'Well, if that isn't what you like, what *would* you like to do?' I said, 'Give me a couple weeks and I'll show you. We had some sketches and were ready to go, but we weren't able to build it until he took over."

What Telnak and Design Executive John Aiken (who had supervised the '67-'70 Cougar's design) showed him two weeks later was, in fact, a concept model of what was to have been a future Lincoln luxury coupe. "It was basically a new Mark," says Allen Ornes, then Studio Manager in charge of Thunderbird/Cougar design, "but taking the approach of an aerodynamic luxury car. It had no program, no model year; it was just something we had worked out in the studio. Jack put the eggcrate grille and T-Bird lettering on it and rolled it into a weekend showing here at the Design Center." The rest, as they say, is history. Petersen loved the "Luxury Aero Coupe," and it was soon being fashioned into the '83 Thunderbird. A modified longer-wheelbase version with Lincoln Mark cues was similarly becoming the sleek '84 Mark VII. And a new and different Cougar was derived from it as well.

"After we had the more functional approach pretty well in place," Ornes says, "and as the new T-Bird was being developed and coming along, we obviously had to come up with a Cougar derivative. And we wanted to give it a more formal and, I guess, more sophisticated approach—something that would be seen as a little more expensive. Obviously the roof . . . did that. It helped achieve our main marketing goal, which was maximum differential from the Thunderbird, and it helped the car fit into Lincoln-Mercury showrooms and serve their tradition, which is usually upscale and conservative."

The new Cougar's roofline *was* certainly striking. It combined a severely vertical backlight with a reverse-curve leading edge on the C-pillar. "The designer who came up with that theme," Ornes continues, "was my assistant at the time, Gary Haas. We originally had a little more angle coming off the belt, but we were not able to sell that. Some people thought we were going too far, and a lot of them would have been happy to keep the . . . parallel-angled C-pillar from the '80-'82 Cougar."

A more aerodynamic and contemporary version of the traditional Cougar face—a vertical-textured stand-up grille between dual horizontal headlamps and integrated parking and side marker lights—was developed for the front, while the same "updated traditional" thinking led to horizontal wraparound tail lamps and a slight Cougar "hump" in back. "We had a completely different overall shape," Ornes explains, "and aerodynamic characteristics that were much different from any previous Cougar. But we did try to pick up ornamentation and detail cues from the past so that it had some heritage." Common features of the slippery new Thunderbird/Cougar body included its sharply sloping hood and windshield, innovative "limousine-style" doors that wrapped up into the roof, and concealed drip rails. Unfortunately, the new interior design was handicapped by its necessary use of carryover parts from the previous T-Bird/Cougar. It turned out more family sedan than sporty coupe and a lot more "old" Ford than new, and it had no provision for driver-oriented instrumentation or a tachometer. But lead times and budgets being what they were, that problem would have to be dealt with later.

Since the new Thunderbird and Cougar were based on an extensively modified and updated version of the old Fairmont/Zephyr platform, the engineering task was more development than design oriented. "We completely redid the car for 1983," says Jim Kennedy, who headed the Mid-Size and Specialty Car Development Group at the time. "With the new styling, we were able to take a little different approach to begin with, and I think we've improved on it every year since. We definitely had direction from Mr. Petersen to make it more of a driver's car, which was a refreshing change for us.

"When you re-skin a car like that, everything changes. You change the whole greenhouse and all the structure changes. The concept was basically the same, but it had a new floorpan and very few carryover components. That gave us the opportunity to make a lot of changes that we felt would be beneficial. We put a lot of new ideas into it—structural adhesives, for example—and other things that had not been used before. We had a lot of conflicting objectives: cost, weight, performance, economy, and the various dynamic objectives. And some of the older management didn't change their wants. Yes, they wanted it to handle and steer better; but they still wanted the old soft ride. That made it much more of a challenge, and there were compromises made; but in the end I think we satisfied everyone fairly well."

They certainly did. The '83 Thunderbird and Cougar reached showrooms in February, 1983, and (surprisingly, to many people) the Cougar became an instant hit. While the T-Bird's smoothly rounded contours seemed radical at first to conservative Americans, it soon began to catch on as well and would eventually surpass the Cougar in sales . . . but not by much. The brilliance of the program as a whole, it turned out, was having two so completely different versions of the same basic car that they split the public almost right down the center. Everyone seemed to love one and hate the other, and few were undecided.

Functionally, though, the difference was very slight. They shared the same 3.8-liter V-6 engine with standard three-speed and optional four-speed automatic transmissions. Both also shared the same shortened wheelbase (to 104 inches from '82's 108.4 inches) modified Fairmont/Zephyr platform and crisp-handling, smooth-riding suspension, which was little-changed in design from the previous year but fine-tuned and greatly improved by standard nitrogen-pressurized shocks front and rear. And both shared the same basic instrument panel and interior, in base and uplevel trim.

The differences were primarily in the front and rear appearance and, of course, the roof, which not only set the Cougar apart but also gave it slightly better rear-seat headroom and decreased its drag coefficient from the T-Bird's impressive (for 1983) .35 to a more Mercury-like .40. Individual reclining seats in luxurious "Manhattan" cloth, a full-length console with a stowage bin, door panel bins, a soft-trim luxury woodtone steering wheel, a deep-well trunk, an analog quartz clock and a 21-gallon fuel tank were standard. Major new options included P205 tires on polycast wheels, power outside mirrors, an anti-theft alarm system, six-way power seats, clear-coat metallic paint and such dated holdovers as "coach" lamps and a partial vinyl roof cap.

Fuel prices had stabilized and even dropped a bit by then, so the 130-horse 5.0-liter V-8 was restored as a Cougar option later that year. *Motor Trend* tested a V-8-powered Cougar LS that summer, and the resulting September 1983 report was subtitled "Quality and paradox in a fine personal coupe." "The Cougar shows intelligent design and sound execution," wrote then Executive Editor Kevin Smith, "diluted in crucial ways by odd and inexplicable little flaws." The magazine found the V-8/four-speed automatic powertrain sweet in nature but disappointingly thirsty given its so-so 11.3-second 0–60 performance. It called the ride and handling "exemplary" on smooth roads but found the rear axle badly undercontrolled on rougher surfaces and in sharp transitional maneuvers.

Like nearly everyone else who reviewed it, *Motor Trend* also criticized the Cougar's roof and rear-deck shapes as subjectively unappealing and inconsistent with the rest of the car's cleanly sculpted lines. It found the interior, if not exciting, at least comfortable, quiet and of excellent quality in fit and materials. But Smith criticized the front seats' "loose-pillow" design for creating a torturous pressure point in most occupants' backs.

The next year brought a new-concept XR-7, the Cougar counterpart to Ford's fast, fine-looking and fine-handling new Thunderbird Turbo Coupe. For the first time, the XR-7 label stood for driving fun, excitement and performance instead of (as one writer once put it) "a Cougar in a sport jacket." This XR-7 was powered by a surprisingly strong electronically fuel-injected, 2.3-liter turbocharged four-cylinder engine, a modern derivative of an old overhead-cam Pinto unit given new life and muscle by Ford's Special Vehicle Operations (SVO) racing department. It also featured a well-developed handling-oriented suspension (complete with the Mustang GT's four-shock arrangement for rear axle control), serious P205/70HR14 performance tires on handsome alloy wheels, and a choice of five-speed manual or three-speed automatic transmission.

The '84 XR-7 was available in a choice of four specific paint combinations, all set off by a gray "tri-band" lower body stripe and silver-metallic painted polycast wheels. Interior trim, including the special, multi-adjustable sport seats, was tasteful charcoal and gray. Also included in the package were power windows, a tachometer and a leather-wrapped four-spoke steering wheel. For the rest of the line, the V-6 engine (like the V-8 and turbo four) got electronic fuel injection, and all three were newly managed by the company's fourth-generation electronic engine control system, EEC IV. Dual fluidic washer nozzles replaced the previous single nozzle on each wiper arm, counterbalanced hood springs replaced the '83's prop rod, a new "A-frame" deluxe steering wheel (with center horn-blow) became standard, and a handy low-oil-level light was added to the optional diagnostic warning system.

Nineteen-eighty-five brought a minor facelift front and rear. The grille texture changed, the tail lamps were redone with smoked glass and a more flush surface, and both standard wheelcovers and optional alloy wheels were redesigned. Of far greater importance, however, was the new instrument panel, which was more contemporary and also more consistent with the exterior style and image. A choice of three different instrument sets was offered: standard, with digital speedometer and odometer; full electronic; or (for the XR-7) a full analog cluster. Other significant features included side window defoggers and positive-closing air conditioning registers.

Standard seating changed to a 60/40 split bench with a consolette (in place of individual seats with a full console), P205/70R14 whitewall tires became standard, and body corrosion protection was improved. The XR-7's turbocharged engine got more power, thanks to higher-flow fuel injectors and electronic boost control, and its optional five-speed shifter was modified for shorter, crisper throws. Power seat recliners, a headlamp convenience group (including Autolamp and automatic dimmer) and a stereo graphic equalizer were added to the option choices; the automatic climate control went full electronic; and the optional cassette tape decks were upgraded.

Cougar's model lineup (standard GS, luxury LS and high-performance XR-7) remained unchanged for '86, as did the styling, except for new colors and addition of a federally mandated high-center brake lamp on the rear package tray. The base tire size grew to P215/70R14, available with black or white sidewalls, and the rear seat cushion was modified to better accommodate a center rear passenger. A collapsible space-saving spare tire was the only important new option, but a power Moonroof was promised for later in the year. Most significantly, the optional V-8 was replaced by a higher-tech version with sequential multi-port injection; and the four-speed overdrive automatic became available as an option with the standard V-6.

As this is written early in 1987, the new-generation Thunderbird and Cougar have just undergone their first *major* facelift. The overall shapes are barely changed, but both are longer, smoother and sleeker. The T-Bird is slightly more aerodynamic (.34 vs. the previous .35 Cd), but the Cougar's striking shape is substantially lower in drag at .36 compared to the previous model's .40.

This redesign program (according to former Studio Manager David Turner) was late off the mark, but the use of new high-tech computer graphics techniques helped complete it on time. "We did the roof and the front end on the tube right from a sketch and a tape rendering," Turner explains, "then went straight to computer-generated surface development. We then machine milled those surfaces in full-size clay, smoothed them out by hand, and had a finished model for approval." They skipped the time-consuming process of hand-forming of a clay model from designers' sketches and full-size tape drawings.

Turner's direction was essentially to refine it without changing the original's successful formula. "We knew what was happening in the marketplace," he says, "so our job was to reinforce that reputation, make it [the car] more aerodynamic and improve on it in fit and finish, mechanically and in any way we could—to hold onto the theme, yet make it more contemporary for the late Eighties. We took the basic theme of the grille and set it in flush between new aerodynamic headlights. We gave it flush side glass, a higher rear end and more of a wedge-shaped profile, and we took off that sculpture on the rear deck. The leading edge of the C-pillar has a more pronounced curve at its leading edge, the backlight and tail lamps are flush, and the rear half of the roof is much softer than before for better aerodynamics."

The engineering goal, as before, was continued development. "We

made a lot of improvements from '83 to '85," Kennedy says. "Then it started to get exciting. The longer you work on something, the better you can make it. After a while, after you've learned how the hardware reacts and responds and you start making progress, it's surprising how far you can go. We began to see the opportunity to make a really super car out of it. That is why '87 is really exciting to us, because now we're getting to the potential of that platform."

The turbo engine, never as popular in the more conservative Cougar as in the hot T-Bird Turbo Coupe, fell off the powertrain list for '87, but the fuel-injected V-8 replaced it as standard XR-7 engine. The more efficient four-speed overdrive automatic replaced the old three-speed as the standard Cougar transmission, while new front suspension geometry and variable-rate springs front and rear improved ride, handling, steering and NVH, and a new fast-fill brake master-cylinder was added to enhance braking performance. Also, as part of the overall upgrade program, the previous lower-line GS model was dropped.

Inside the cabin were new door trim panels, a new two-spoke steering wheel (replacing the previous A-frame design), a molded headliner, new individual bucket seats and a shortened console (to improve legroom for a rear-center passenger), plus softer colors for the instrument panel (to reduce reflection in the windshield) and matching console or consolette. Power windows returned to optional status (they were briefly standard in '86), but air conditioning and tinted glass became standard.

Finally, to celebrate Cougar's hard-earned 20th birthday and its recent success, a special 20th Anniversary Editon was unveiled in January 1987. A year-long effort supervised by Senior Designer Jerry Senior, it featured a distinctive medium cabernet (wine) exterior color with gold accents, plus "virtually every luxury and convenience item a buyer could want," according to Lincoln-Mercury General Manager and Ford Vice President Thomas J. Wagner. The only available options were the keyless entry system and a power moonroof.

"We wanted a car that would set an image for the buyer," Senior

**1984 Cougar LS, owned by Deanie Winter**

explains, "a car that would let people know that he'd spent some extra dollars for something very special. We ended up with cloisonné and gold embellishments. All of the nomenclature on the car is in gold—the first time we've ever done cloisonné nameplates that are actually gold-plated. The anniversary badges on the decklid and C-pillars are done the same way. Gold-plating has never passed our laboratory standards before, but we were able to work with our lab and got it approved for this specific project.

"The interior is done in a high-series Thunderbird leather style in a perforated ultra-suede material that was developed specifically for use in this car. The seats are piped in medium cabernet, and the seating surfaces are a sand beige color with red cabernet accents. The anniversary logo is also repeated in a set of specially made embroidered floormats.

"There is a very, very fine line between embellishing tastefully and doing it in a garish manner," Senior adds. "We put things on and took

*1986 Cougar LS, owned by Ford Motor Company*

things off and went through a lot of soul-searching in everything we did. We wanted this car to have a very recognizable look. We didn't want someone to spend a lot of money on it and then see his neighbor down the block driving an ordinary Cougar that looked very similar. Yet we tried to accomplish that in good taste. I think we have."

The 20th Anniversary Cougar went on sale in February 1987. Just 5,400 were built—5,000 for the U.S. market and 400 more for Canada. The price: $18,052. From this vantage point, even as the sales pace slows at the top of a five-year industry recovery, it looks to be another of many good years to come for Mercury's renewed Cougar.

**1987 Cougar 20th Anniversary Edition, owned by Ford Motor Company**

# APPENDICES

## ENGINE SPECIFICATIONS

| YEAR | TYPE | DISPLACEMENT (CU. IN.) | BORE & STROKE | CARB | COMP. RATIO | BRAKE HP @ RPM | TORQUE (LBS.-FT). @ RPM |
|---|---|---|---|---|---|---|---|
| 1967 | | | | | | | |
| | V-8 ohv | 289 | 4.00x2.87 | 2x1 | 9.3:1 | 200 @ 4400 | 282 @ 2400 |
| | V-8 ohv | 289 | 4.00x2.87 | 4x1 | 9.8:1 | 225 @ 4800 | 305 @ 3200 |
| | V-8 ohv | 390 | 4.05x3.78 | 4x1 | 10.5:1 | 320 @ 4800 | 427 @ 3200 |
| 1968 | | | | | | | |
| | V-8 ohv | 289 | 4.00x2.87 | 2x1 | 8.7:1 | 195 @ 4600 | 288 @ 2600 |
| | V-8 ohv | 302 | 4.00x3.00 | 2x1 | 9.0:1 | 210 @ 4600 | 300 @ 2600 |
| | V-8 ohv | 302 | 4.00x3.00 | 4x1 | 10.0:1 | 230 @ 4800 | 310 @ 2800 |
| | V-8 ohv | 390 | 4.05x3.78 | 2x1 | 10.5:1 | 280 @ 4400 | 403 @ 2600 |
| | V-8 ohv | 390 | 4.05x3.78 | 4x1 | 10.5:1 | 325 @ 4800 | 427 @ 3200 |
| | V-8 ohv | 427 | 4.23x3.78 | 4x1 | 10.9:1 | 390 @ 5600 | 460 @ 3200 |
| | V-8 ohv | 428 | 4.13x3.98 | 4x1 | 10.6:1 | 335 @ 5400 | 440 @ 3400 |
| 1969 | | | | | | | |
| | V-8 ohv | 351 | 4.00x3.50 | 2x1 | 9.5:1 | 250 @ 4600 | 355 @ 2600 |
| | V-8 ohv | 351 | 4.00x3.50 | 4x1 | 10.7:1 | 290 @ 4800 | 385 @ 3200 |
| | V-8 ohv | 390 | 4.05x3.78 | 4x1 | 10.5:1 | 320 @ 4600 | 427 @ 3200 |
| | V-8 ohv | 428 | 4.13x3.98 | 4x1 | 10.6:1 | 335 @ 5200 | 440 @ 3400 |
| | V-8 ohv | 302 | 4.00x3.00 | 4x1 | 10.5:1 | 290 @ 5800 | 290 @ 4300 |
| 1970 | | | | | | | |
| | V-8 ohv | 351 | 4.00x3.50 | 2x1 | 9.5:1 | 250 @ 4600 | 355 @ 2600 |
| | V-8 ohv | 351 | 4.00x3.50 | 4x1 | 11.0:1 | 300 @ 5400 | 380 @ 3400 |
| | V-8 ohv | 428 (CJ) | 4.13x3.98 | 4x1 | 10.6:1 | 335 @ 5200 | 440 @ 3400 |
| | V-8 ohv | 302 (HO) | 4.00x3.00 | 4x1 | 10.6:1 | 290 @ 5800 | 290 @ 4300 |
| 1971 | | | | | | | |
| | V-8 ohv | 351 | 4.00x3.50 | 2x1 | 9.0:1 | 240 @ 4600 | 350 @ 2600 |
| | V-8 ohv | 351 (CJ) | 4.00x3.50 | 4x1 | 9.0:1 | 280 @ 5800 | 345 @ 3800 |
| | V-8 ohv | 351 | 4.00x3.50 | 4x1 | 10.7:1 | 285 @ 5400 | 370 @ 3400 |
| | V-8 ohv | 429 (CJ) | 4.36x3.59 | 4x1 | 11.3:1 | 370 @ 5400 | 450 @ 3400 |
| 1972 | | | | | | | |
| | V-8 ohv | 351 | 4.00x3.50 | 2x1 | 8.6:1 | 164 @ 4000 | 276 @ 2000 |
| | V-8 ohv | 351 | 4.00x3.50 | 4x1 | 8.6:1 | 262 @ 5400 | 299 @ 3600 |
| | V-8 ohv | 351 (CJ) | 4.00x3.50 | 4x1 | 8.6:1 | 266 @ 5400 | 301 @ 3600 |
| 1973 | | | | | | | |
| | V-8 ohv | 351 | 4.00x3.50 | 2x1 | 8.0:1 | 168 @ 4000 | 256 @ 2400 |
| | V-8 ohv | 351 | 4.00x3.50 | 4x1 | 7.9:1 | 264 @ 4800 | 314 @ 3600 |
| 1974 | | | | | | | |
| | V-8 ohv | 351 (W) | 4.00x3.50 | 2x1 | 8.0:1 | 162 @ 4000 | 275 @ 2200 |
| | V-8 ohv | 351 (C) | 4.00x3.50 | 2x1 | 8.0:1 | 163 @ 4200 | 278 @ 2000 |
| | V-8 ohv[1] | 351 | 4.00x3.50 | 4x1 | 7.9:1 | 255 @ 5600 | 290 @ 3400 |
| | V-8 ohv | 400 | 4.00x4.00 | 2x1 | 8.0:1 | 170 @ 3400 | 330 @ 2000 |
| | V-8 ohv | 460 | 4.36x3.85 | 4x1 | 8.0:1 | 220 @ 4000 | 355 @ 2600 |
| 1975 | | | | | | | |
| | V-8 ohv[1] | 351 (M) | 4.00x3.50 | 2x1 | 8.0:1 | 148 @ 3800 | 243 @ 2400 |
| | V-8 ohv[2] | 351 (M) | 4.00x3.50 | 2x1 | 8.0:1 | 150 @ 3800 | 244 @ 2800 |
| | V-8 ohv[1] | 351 (W) | 4.00x3.50 | 2x1 | 8.0:1 | 154 @ 3800 | 268 @ 2200 |
| | V-8 ohv[1] | 400 | 4.00x4.00 | 2x1 | 8.0:1 | 158 @ 3800 | 276 @ 2000 |
| | V-8 ohv[2] | 400 | 4.00x4.00 | 2x1 | 8.0:1 | 144 @ 3600 | 255 @ 2200 |
| | V-8 ohv[1] | 460 | 4.36x3.85 | 4x1 | 8.0:1 | 216 @ 4000 | 366 @ 2600 |
| | V-8 ohv[2] | 460 | 4.36x3.85 | 4x1 | 8.0:1 | 217 @ 4000 | 365 @ 2600 |
| 1976 | | | | | | | |
| | V-8 ohv | 351 (M) | 4.00x3.50 | 2x1 | 8.0:1 | 152 @ 3800 | 274 @ 1600 |
| | V-8 ohv[1] | 351 (W) | 4.00x3.50 | 2x1 | 8.0:1 | 154 @ 3400 | 286 @ 1800 |
| | V-8 ohv | 400 | 4.00x4.00 | 2x1 | 8.0:1 | 180 @ 3800 | 336 @ 1800 |
| | V-8 ohv | 460 | 4.36x3.85 | 4x1 | 8.0:1 | 202 @ 3800 | 352 @ 1600 |
| 1977 | | | | | | | |
| | V-8 ohv[1] | 302 | 4.00x3.00 | 2x1 | 8.4:1 | 130 @ 3400 | 243 @ 1800 |
| | V-8 ohv[1] | 351 (W) | 4.00x3.50 | 2x1 | 8.3:1 | 149 @ 3200 | 291 @ 1600 |
| | V-8 ohv | 351 (M) | 4.00x3.50 | 2x1 | 8.0:1 | 161 @ 3600 | 285 @ 1800 |
| | V-8 ohv[1] | 400 | 4.00x4.00 | 2x1 | 8.0:1 | 173 @ 3800 | 326 @ 1600 |
| | V-8 ohv[2] | 400 | 4.00x4.00 | 2x1 | 8.0:1 | 168 @ 3800 | 323 @ 1600 |
| 1978 | | | | | | | |
| | V-8 ohv[1] | 302 | 4.00x3.00 | 2x1 | 8.4:1 | 135 @ 3400 | 248 @ 1700 |
| | V-8 ohv[1] | 351 (W) | 4.00x3.50 | 2x1 | 8.3:1 | 143 @ 3200 | 267 @ 1700 |
| | V-8 ohv | 351 (M) | 4.00x3.50 | 2x1 | 8.0:1 | 143 @ 3200 | 267 @ 1700 |
| | V-8 ohv | 400 | 4.00x4.00 | 2x1 | 8.0:1 | 153 @ 3600 | 278 @ 1900 |
| 1979 | | | | | | | |
| | V-8 ohv[1] | 302 | 4.00x3.00 | 2x1 | 8.4:1 | 133 @ 3400 | 245 @ 1600 |
| | V-8 ohv[1] | 351 (W) | 4.00x3.50 | 2x1 | 8.3:1 | 135 @ 3200 | 286 @ 1400 |
| | V-8 ohv[1] | 351 (M) | 4.00x3.50 | 2x1 | 8.0:1 | 151 @ 3600 | 270 @ 2200 |
| | V-8 ohv[2] | 351 (M) | 4.00x3.50 | 2x1 | 8.0:1 | 149 @ 3800 | 258 @ 2200 |

# BASIC SPECIFICATIONS

| | 1967 | 1968 | 1969 | 1970 | 1971 | 1972 | 1973 | 1974 | 1975 | 1976 | 1977 | 1978 | 1979 | 1980 | 1981 | 1982 | 1983 | 1984 | 1985 | 1986 | 1987 |
|---|---|---|---|---|---|---|---|---|---|---|---|---|---|---|---|---|---|---|---|---|---|
| Wheelbase (ins.) | 111.0 | 111.0 | 111.0 | 111.1 | 112.1 | 112.1 | 112.1 | 114.0 | 114.0 | 114.0 | 114.0 | 114.0 | 114.0 | 108.4 | 108.4 | 108.4 | 104.0 | 104.0 | 104.0 | 104.0 | 104.2 |
| Overall Length (ins.) | 190.3 | 190.3 | 193.8 | 196.1 | 196.7 | 196.7 | 199.7 | 215.5 | 215.5 | 215.7 | 215.5 | 215.5 | 215.5 | 200.4 | 200.4 | 200.4 | 197.6 | 197.6 | 197.6 | 197.6 | 200.8 |
| Overall Height (ins.) | 51.8 | 51.7 | 51.5 | 51.3 | 50.8 | 50.8 | 50.7 | 52.5 | 52.6 | 52.6 | 52.6 | 52.6 | 52.8 | 53.0 | 53.2 | 53.2 | 53.4 | 53.4 | 53.4 | 53.4 | 53.8 |
| Overall Width (ins.) | 71.2 | 71.3 | 74.2 | 74.2 | 75.1 | 75.1 | 75.1 | 78.5 | 78.5 | 78.5 | 78.0 | 78.6 | 78.6 | 74.1 | 74.1 | 74.1 | 71.1 | 71.1 | 71.1 | 71.1 | 71.1 |
| Front Tread (ins.) | 58.1 | 58.5 | 58.5 | 58.5 | 61.5 | 61.5 | 61.5 | 63.4 | 63.4 | 63.4 | 63.6 | 63.2 | 63.2 | 58.1 | 58.1 | 58.1 | 58.1 | 58.1 | 58.1 | 58.1 | 58.1 |
| Rear Tread (ins.) | 58.1 | 58.5 | 58.5 | 58.5 | 61.0 | 61.0 | 60.8 | 63.5 | 63.5 | 63.5 | 63.5 | 63.1 | 63.1 | 57.0 | 57.0 | 57.0 | 58.5 | 58.5 | 58.5 | 58.5 | 58.5 |
| Curb Weight (lbs.) | 3119 | 3230 | 3402 | 3431 | 3430 | 3460 | 3558 | 4262 | 4351 | 4376 | 4030 | 3946 | 4012 | 3270 | 3259 | 3152 | 3099 | 3065 | 3084 | 3085 | 3133 |
| Trunk Space (cu. ft.) | 9.1 | 9.2 | 10.2 | 10.2 | 10.4 | 10.4 | 10.4 | 16.5 | 16.5 | 16.5 | 15.4 | 15.9 | 15.7 | 17.7 | 17.7 | 17.7 | 14.6 | 14.6 | 14.6 | 14.6 | 14.6 |
| Fuel Capacity (gals.) | 17.0 | 17.0 | 20.0 | 20.0 | 20.0 | 19.5 | 19.5 | 26.5 | 26.5 | 26.5 | 26.5 | 21.0 | 21.0 | 17.5 | 18.0 | 21.0 | 21.0 | 20.6 | 20.6 | 22.1 | 22.1 |
| Base List Price ($) | 2,851 | 2,910 | 3,016 | 3,114 | 3,289 | 3,061 | 3,372 | 4,301 | 5,153 | 5,125 | 5,274 | 5,603 | 5,994 | 6,569 | 7,799 | 9,508 | 9,953 | 10,410 | 11,082 | 11,853 | 14,062 |

Note: In model years 1977-79 and 1981-82, when coupe, sedan and station wagon models were in the lineup, specifications are provided for the XR-7 coupe only.

**1980**
| | | | | | | | |
|---|---|---|---|---|---|---|---|
| L-6 ohv | 200 | 3.68x3.13 | 1x1 | 8.6:1 | 94 @ 4000 | 157 @ 2000 |
| V-8 ohv | 255 | 3.68x3.00 | 2x1 | 8.8:1 | 115 @ 3800 | 191 @ 2000 |
| V-8 ohv | 302 | 4.00x3.00 | 2x1 | 8.4:1 | 131 @ 3600 | 231 @ 1600 |

**1981**
| | | | | | | |
|---|---|---|---|---|---|---|
| L-6 ohv | 200 | 3.68x3.13 | 1x1 | 8.6:1 | 88 @ 3800 | 154 @ 1400 |
| V-8 ohv | 255 | 3.68x3.00 | 2x1 | 8.2:1 | 115 @ 3800 | 195 @ 2200 |
| V-8 ohv | 302 | 4.00x3.00 | 2x1 | 8.4:1 | 140 @ 3400 | 235 @ 1600 |

**1982**
| | | | | | | |
|---|---|---|---|---|---|---|
| L-6 ohv | 200 | 3.68x3.13 | 1x1 | 8.6:1 | 87 @ 3800 | 154 @ 1400 |
| V-6 ohv | 232 | 3.80x3.40 | 2x1 | 8.8:1 | 112 @ 4000 | 175 @ 2600 |
| V-8 ohv | 255 | 3.68x3.00 | 2x1 | 8.2:1 | 111 @ 3400 | 194 @ 1600 |

**1983**
| | | | | | | |
|---|---|---|---|---|---|---|
| V-6 ohv | 232 | 3.80x3.40 | 2x1 | 8.6:1 | 110 @ 3800 | 175 @ 2200 |
| V-8 ohv | 302 | 4.00x3.00 | TBI | 8.4:1 | 130 @ 3200 | 240 @ 2000 |

**1984**
| | | | | | | |
|---|---|---|---|---|---|---|
| V-6 | 232 | 3.80x3.40 | TBI | 8.7:1 | 120 @ 3600 | 205 @ 1600 |
| V-8 | 302 | 4.00x3.00 | TBI | 8.4:1 | 140 @ 3200 | 250 @ 1600 |
| L-4 sohc | 140(T) | 3.78x3.12 | MPI | 8.0:1 | 145 @ 4600 | 180 @ 3600 |

**1985**
| | | | | | | |
|---|---|---|---|---|---|---|
| V-6 ohv | 232 | 3.80x3.40 | TBI | 8.7:1 | 120 @ 3600 | 205 @ 1600 |
| V-8 ohv | 302 | 4.00x3.00 | TBI | 8.4:1 | 140 @ 3200 | 250 @ 1600 |
| L-4 sohc | 140 (T)[3] | 3.78x3.12 | MPI | 8.0:1 | 155 @ 4600 | 190 @ 2800 |
| L-4 sohc | 140 (T)[4] | 3.78x3.12 | MPI | 8.0:1 | 145 @ 4400 | 180 @ 3000 |

**1986**
| | | | | | | |
|---|---|---|---|---|---|---|
| V-6 ohv | 232 | 3.80x3.40 | TBI | 8.7:1 | 120 @ 3600 | 205 @ 1600 |
| V-8 ohv | 302 | 4.00x3.00 | MPI | 8.9:1 | 150 @ 3400 | 270 @ 2000 |
| L-4 sohc | 140 (T)[3] | 3.78x3.12 | MPI | 8.0:1 | 155 @ 4600 | 190 @ 2800 |
| L-4 sohc | 140 (T)[4] | 3.78x3.12 | MPI | 8.0:1 | 145 @ 4400 | 180 @ 3000 |

**1987**
| | | | | | | |
|---|---|---|---|---|---|---|
| V-6 ohv | 232 | 3.80x3.40 | TBI | 8.7:1 | 120 @ 3600 | 205 @ 1600 |
| V-8 ohv | 302 | 4.00x3.00 | MPI | 8.9:1 | 150 @ 3200 | 270 @ 2000 |

| | | | |
|---|---|---|---|
| 1 | Not available in California | HO | High Output |
| 2 | California only | M | Modified |
| 3 | 5-speed manual transmission | MPI | Multi Port Injection |
| 4 | Automatic transmission | T | Turbo |
| C | Cleveland | TBI | Throttle Body Injection |
| CJ | Cobra Jet | W | Windsor |

# MODEL YEAR PRODUCTION

| | | COUGAR | COUGAR XR-7 | TOTAL |
|---|---|---|---|---|
| 1967 | Coupe | 123,672 | 27,221 | 150,893 |
| 1968 | Coupe | 81,014 | 32,712 | 113,726 |
| 1969 | Coupe | 66,331 | 23,918 | |
| | Convertible | 5,796 | 4,024 | 100,069 |
| 1970 | Coupe | 49,479 | 18,565 | |
| | Convertible | 2,322 | 1,977 | 72,363 |
| 1971 | Coupe | 34,008 | 25,416 | |
| | Convertible | 1,723 | 1,717 | 62,864 |
| 1972 | Coupe | 23,731 | 26,802 | |
| | Convertible | 1,240 | 1,929 | 53,702 |
| 1973 | Coupe | 21,069 | 35,110 | |
| | Convertible | 1,284 | 3,165 | 60,628 |
| 1974 | Coupe | — | 91,670 | 91,670 |
| 1975 | Coupe | — | 62,987 | 62,987 |
| 1976 | Coupe | — | 83,765 | 83,765 |
| 1977 | Coupe | 70,024 | 124,799 | 194,823 |
| 1978 | Coupe | 46,762 | 166,508 | 213,270 |
| 1979 | Coupe | 8,436 | 163,716 | 172,152 |
| 1980 | Coupe | | 58,028 | 58,028 |
| 1981 | Coupe | 53,653 | 37,275 | 90,928 |
| 1982 | Coupe | 56,950 | 16,867 | 73,817 |
| 1983 | Coupe | 75,743 | | 75,743 |
| 1984 | Coupe | 125,019 | 6,171 | 131,190 |
| 1985 | Coupe | 109,414 | 7,860 | 117,274 |
| 1986 | Coupe | 129,400 | 6,504 | 135,904 |

# PHOTO CREDITS

*Color photography by Roy D. Query: cover, pp. 8-9, 12, 20-21, 25, 26-27, 29, 36-37, 56-57. Color photography by Leslie Bird: pp. 35, 52-53, 54-55. Color photography by Bill Sumner: pp. 32-33. All remaining color photography courtesy Ford Motor Company.*

*Black-and-white photography pg. 24 (top) by Alice Bixler, courtesy* Road & Track; *pg. 24 (bottom) by Cam Warren, courtesy* Road & Track. *All remaining black-and-white photography courtesy Ford Motor Company.*